VIA Folios 168

Extinction Wednesday

Cover Image: 1800s Bikes in Vines, mural by Nicole Cherry. Cover photograph of 1800s Bikes in Vines by Mary Elizabeth Sullivan.

Library of Congress Control Number: 2023952516

Published by
BORDIGHERA PRESS
John D. Calandra Italian American Institute
25 W. 43rd Street, 17th Floor
New York, NY 10036

VIA Folios 168
ISBN 978-1-59954-215-7

EXTINCTION WEDNESDAY

Joey Nicoletti

BORDIGHERA PRESS

.

Contents

For Beth, Max, Stella Bella, and Roxy,
for absolutely everything.

Do you like having a good time?
Then you need a good watch!

SYLVESTER STALLONE

The world is full of terrible & beautiful mutations
Like a pearl is by-product of disease
You're not done with your transformations.

MARISA FRASCA

May Stars

Rona. The coronavirus. By any name, the COVID-19 pandemic has given rise to more adversity and challenges than some might have ever imagined, including quarantine. Fortunately for me, I am a homebody. One of the best parts of staying home is that my partner Beth and I get to spend more time with our fur-babies: Max, our short-haired cat, Stella Bella, our Boston terrier, and Roxy, our miniature poodle, who is the most recent addition to our family.

Roxy came to us from a puppy mill in Ohio, via our local ASPCA shelter. When Beth and I filled out Roxy's adoption papers, we were informed that she has luxating patellas: loose knees in all of her legs. Her back patellas are particularly tricky, and her leg muscles were thin we met her, on account of not being to stand up fully in her cramped mill cart, and not getting the opportunity to walk or run around often. Having given birth to many puppies, the people of her mill decided that she wouldn't be able to produce more poodles, which, coupled with her tricky knees, apparently made her expendable. Roxy had just arrived at the shelter when we met her, the front of her right ankle shaved from where veterinarians injected her with various medications. Her eyes were glazed, but they seemed to widen as we saw her in her partition. Beth and I were smitten and determined to make her part of our family.

Beth and I aren't surgeons, but Roxy's back legs have become sinewy with time and regular exercise. In the months before COVID-19 became widespread in the USA, the expression in her eyes changed from scared to joyous. She prances when Beth and I take her on walks;

she runs as top speed when she plays with Max and Stella Bella; her eyes widen when she chews a new plush toy; her mouth is open and her tongue sticks out when me, Beth, or both of us are in the kitchen. She also likes to sit in mine or Beth's laps whenever possible, especially when we watch shows or movies together. As a result, this has become a singular joy of quarantine life: watching movies with Roxy, and no screening has been more joyous for me than the one we had for *E.T.: The Extra-Terrestrial,* which took place on a clear, star-studded night, and frogs were croaking with glee in the tall grass beyond my building. Roxy's tail seemed to wag in anticipation, perhaps because she sensed my passion for *E.T.*

One of Roxy's quirks is her temper. She has no qualms about snarling when she doesn't like something. One case in point is Donald Trump. She could be having the time of her life with her siblings or a new toy, but if she hears Trump speaking on TV or hears his voice, she growls and releases shrill Kyries of barks until me or Beth changes the channel. When we watched *E.T.,* she reserved her Kyries for the faceless G-Men and scientists who were following E.T. in the North California forest and put him and Eliot in their on-the-spot quarantine buildings when both characters were sick and on the precipice of death.

Watching *E.T.* from the comfort of my sofa with Roxy also took me back to 1982, when *E.T.* was first released, which made me think of my mother. She was in her thirties. I was 11. By the time *E.T.* was in theatres, my nuclear family's tradition of going out to dinner and a movie on Saturday nights began to occur with less frequency. Part of this was because my brother was an infant, and my older sister was in the heart of her puberty, which meant, among other things, that she hung out with her friends more often than not. *E.T.* was the first film my mother and I saw together since *Grease,* which was released years earlier. As excited as I was to see it, my mother's eagerness was palpable with a capital E. "It's you, me, and a Steven Spielberg movie. We'll love it," she said.

My mother wasn't wrong. When Roxy and I watched E.T. eat Reese's Pieces, My lips curled into smile. I remembered my mother's thunderous chuckle, filling the theatre after Eliot calls his brother

Michael "Penis breath." I joined her and did my best not spit out my root beer. I failed. E.T., clean up aisle one.

* * *

The scene where Eliot and E.T. ride a bike in mid-air and were silhouetted by the moon always moves me. It is a shield of my childhood. My mother's gasp fills my ears. John Williams' music is a sonorous shield, protecting me from the rona if it dared to set foot in our home. Silver or flat screen: I still can't take my eyes off the screen when I see it. *E.T.,* stay home.

I watched Peter Coyote's sensitive performance of Keys, a scientist, with delight. His efforts to help E.T. is commensurate with his concern for Eliot. In this respect, Keys reminds me of my father when he was well-rested and his belly was filled, especially after a meal of steak, a baked potato, and a bowl of pasta on the side.

The scene where Eliot's and Mike's friends help get E.T. to safety also never fails to move me. I tear up when they meet at a park, beside a metallic unisphere-like climbing structure, patches of grass and dirt on the ground.

As I stared at the TV, it occurred to me that parks don't look like this anymore, with their colorful plastic slides and swing sets; their foamy ground, like the one that Beth, Stella Bella and I checked the last time we visited her brother and his family. 1982 was decades ago, but this is another curious development of the rona: my sense of time has been altered, not just in day-to-day progressions, but also in years. Movies are often forms of time travel for me, and COVID-19 has made me reconsider their importance to me: how they mark what's happening or has happened in the world, as well as my own life, and give me hope that the people who run the world might do a better job. When did foam overtake dirt? When will people stop being scared of each other? When will a vaccine be found? When will the United States of America allow a woman to become its President? E.T., what's next?

The film's last act is simultaneously fun and poignant for me. Stella Bella and Beth joined Roxy and I in our living room when E.T. lifts Eliot's, Michael's and their friends BMX bikes into the air, and they pedal in the last light of a striking, fire-red sun. This is the scene of the film that I enjoy the most, because of the togetherness of the characters. Friends and family become one in the same at this moment of the film. E.T. does Eliot's and Mike's friends a solid, because he appreciates the fact that they're trying to help him out. He feels them as much as his Earth hosts. As I consider this further, I also like this scene because it strikes me as a metaphor for what I want to see from United States leadership: acknowledgement. A willingness to put differences aside for the betterment of others, and work together without personal interest and dedicate themselves to containing COVID-19 with competence and confirmed information, as opposed to bluster and braggadocio.

As Eliot and company pedaled in the air, I looked in Roxy's eyes and saw this possibility—however remote—even more so. The kind expression in her dark pupils said to me what quarantined people across Italy had said in signs and their songs sung from balconies: andra tutto bené. Everything will be ok. As loved as I felt in this moment, knowing that this occurred in the presence of Beth and Stella Bella lifted my spirits as high as E.T., Eliot, Michael and their friends were above silhouetted Redwood trees.

Max made a cameo. He sniffed his dinner: a sea-green plate of Meow Mix Chicken and Liver in Sauce Tender Favorites on the kitchen counter. It remained untouched. He sauntered down the hallway and into our home office.

Another scene that always gets me is when Eliot and company take E.T. to the forest for his trip home. E.T.'s spacecraft lands. As was the case when I was 11, the feels overcame me like water over a sandbar when E.T. says goodbye to everyone. His farewell to Eliot required a life preserver in itself. The haymaker always comes when E.T. places his finger on Eliot's head as he tells him, "I'll be right . . . here."

Unlike other occasions, I didn't need a box of Kleenex. Roxy licked my face dry gently and slowly. She didn't stop until my face was dry as our sofa's arm rests.

As the credits rolled, I picked up some stray some cotton Roxy ripped out of a Scarlet macaw stuffed chew toy. The cotton looked like Kris Kringle beard cuttings. I wondered what a rona holiday season will be like.

I applauded when John Williams' grand musical score played. Then I remembered my mother, speaking of how she missed my brother; that we needed to get home to him, so that everyone could eat dinner on time. This included my father, who finished his bus driving shift when everyone else sat down to dinner. He was scheduled to get off work early. E.T., pass the A-1.

Beth went into the kitchen. Roxy jumped out of my lap and pranced towards Beth, her tail wagging. I looked outside. The May stars were bright and reassured, glistening like resplendent periods to all of the questions I have ever asked or will ever ask; the thought of the rona being contained sooner, rather than later feeling almost as possible as meeting visitors from other worlds and becoming friends with one of them, my hopes croaking in the tallgrass.

Orsogna Woman

The older I get, the more I appreciate my Orsognese heritage. The main reason for this is *Superman: The Movie,* which I first saw with my parents in its initial theatrical run. I was a child. Jimmy Carter was President of the United States; my mother couldn't get enough listens of Billy Joel's album *52ⁿᵈ Street;* I ate my first cannoli and read my weight in comic books, especially *Action Comics,* the title that introduced Superman to the world.

After seeing the promotional posters for *Superman,* which promised, "You'll believe a man can fly," my mother was as eager to see it as I was. She was impressed with Christopher Reeve, the Julliard-trained actor who portrayed Clark Kent/Superman, after reading an article about him in *People Magazine.* She devoured it faster than I could say up, up, and away.

As for *Superman* itself, I was hooked from the jump. The names "Marlon Brando" and "Gene Hackman" appeared, and then swelled into almost 3-D proportions, which was accompanied by a *whoosh* sound, and moved in sync with John Williams' dynamic opening score. When the opening credits got to the screenplay writers, my father's eyes widened at the appearance of Mario Puzo's name.

"Mario Puzo?!?!" he said. "That's the guy who wrote *The Godfather,* Joefish," he said to me. I shrugged my shoulders.

"Don't you see? Superman is *Italian,*" my father said. "This is gonna be a good movie!"

My father wasn't wrong. I enjoyed Gene Hackman's comedic take on Lex Luthor, Glenn Ford's and Phyllis Thaxter's brief, but tender renderings of Jonathan and Martha Kent, Margot Kidder's spunky Lois Lane, Jackie Cooper's crusty Perry White, Marc McClure's sincere Jimmy Olsen, Ned Beatty's studied portrayal of Luthor's incompetent henchman Otis, and Valerie Perrine's no-fool-suffering performance as Eve Teschmacher.

I was also taken with the way director Richard Donner used the film's locations. I was thrilled to see that New York City was among the locales, being the place where I was born, so it augmented the sense of familiarity I already had with Superman's story. In thinking about it now, his decision to cast New York City as Metropolis has become more poignant to me over the years. I see the Twin Towers and the Statue of Liberty as metaphors for the late 1970's, the New York City of my youth, before Lady Liberty's restoration from 1984-1986 and before the towers were first attacked in 1994 and destroyed on 9/11.

My father was also impressed with The Fortress of Solitude. I recall him turning to my mother and asking, "What do you think the property taxes are for that place?"

Then there was the Phantom Zone, the structural counterpoint to the Fortress. As depicted in *Superman,* it is a prison made out of a ginormous mirror. Designed by Jor-El, one of Krypton's leading scientists and Superman's father, one of the Kryptonian elders describes the Phantom Zone as "a living death." It appears in the opening act of the film, when Jor-El and the Krypton High Council find the villains Non, Ursa, and General Zod guilty of treason and sedition, which results in their imprisonment.

The Phantom Zone soared towards the villains and entrapped them. I gasped when the Phantom Zone rotated and hurled off into space, Non's, Ursa's, and Zod's voices muffled, their hands and faces pressed against the glass.

"And you think I'm tough," my father said to me. "Madone."

I remember being fascinated by the fact that *Superman* began this way, because it showed the audience not only a world, but also a culture: its customs and values. As an Italian American male who was not taught the language of my ancestors or any variation of it, watching the Kryptonian Elders made me wonder why my parents refused to do so.

"Ask your mother," my father told me when I asked him. "She's from the old country."

I was confused. "The old country?" I asked.

"She's from Italy, Joefish. Don't you know that?"

I did as my father suggested, and my mother explained.

"I was born in Italy, but I came to America when I was a kid."

"Where in Italy? Rome?"

"No. I'm from a town called Orsogna."

"Where's it at?"

"It's a tiny place, near lots of farms and mountains."

As my mother spoke, I saw Smallville, the agricultural community where Superman grew up as Clark Kent, in my mind's movie screen. I saw Jonathan Kent's death scene, just after reassuring Clark that he was on Earth for "a reason."

Then Martha Kent's voice echoed in my brain as she told the future Man of Steel to "Remember us, son. Always remember us."

I rubbed my eyes. "How come Nonna and Nonno don't speak English as well as you do?"

"Because they didn't have the time to learn it like I did," my mother said. "That's the best I can explain it to you."

I was astounded. Not only was my mother bilingual, she was from multiple places, like Superman himself. I had no idea that I had a superhero for a parent: Orsogna Woman. I wanted to know more.

"Can you teach me Italian, Mom?"

My mother took a deep breath. "I don't know, Joseph," she said. "You were born in America. You have to master English."

"But I want to speak Italian, too."

"You're not listening to me," my mother said.

Then she began to tear up. "As an American, English is *your* language. Learn it well. This conversation is over."

I don't know what particular parts of the film's screenplay Mario Puzo wrote, but it wouldn't surprise me if the scenes between Clark Kent/Superman and Jor-El's projection were his creations. True to Jor-El's words, the son becomes the father, like Michael and Vito Corleone: Michael becomes the Godfather. Small wonder that Marlon Brando, who played Vito Corleone in The Godfather, plays Jor-El in *Superman.*

That he also commanded and received a reported salary of 3.7 million dollars didn't hurt, especially given that it was the most an actor had ever been paid for a film as of 1978. Acting like an Italian American mobster made serious bank. Acting like a Kryptonian scientist made even more. Talk about an offer he couldn't refuse.

My fluency in Italian has improved through the years, which is to say that I can write and speak a few phrases fairly well. I have learned from friends and colleagues mostly, which has also yielded some fascinating and troubling discoveries. Among them, I am related to Charles "The Typewriter" Nicoletti, a notorious Chicago-based hitman, who is also alleged to have been one of the mechanics that shot and killed JFK. This is not exactly truth, justice, or the American way as I saw it portrayed in *Superman* or heard about it from the adults of my family. The reports of The Typewriter's participation in the JFK assassination have not been confirmed, but they strike me as having some emotional truth to them, much like Superman's capacity for love. Watching him turn back time to save Lois Lane feels as if it could actually happen, on account on the depth of his love. The same rings true to me about The Typewriter, whose disregard for life was such that it led to his involvement in multiple murders, in the name of crime family pride, honor, and personal interests.

The elders of my family claim to have not known about The Typewriter, but they have often expressed sympathy for him, especially the men, claiming that, "He was probably driven to it." If anything, many of the men in my family see being a gangster in the same light as being Superman: a model of singular veneration.

I saw this theory in practice at a wedding I attended recently. My cousin was the bride. I was dressed in a navy-blue suit, a purple shirt, and a floral tie. My father, who also attended, had recently been diagnosed with having cataracts. He wore a black polyester polo shirt, black slacks, socks, and shoes. When we left the church, he hugged me.

"Hey! Joefish! You look like a gangster! Sharp."

I raised an eyebrow, advised him to drink less, and walked towards my car. If beauty is in the eye of the beholder, I thought, then my father's cataracts were worse than either of us could have possibly imagined.

The worst part of the exchange was that I knew better. My father did not mean to be offensive any more than Superman meant to forget about Lois Lane when he was trying to save the Earth in his eponymously named movie. Lex Luthor was his enemy. Anyone who was not in good standing with Sam Giancana was The Typewriter's. To my father's way of thinking, being in the mafia is a charmed life. To be a member of a mafia crew—and especially a high ranking one, such as a "made man," also known as a "wiseguy" or a "capo:" the head of a crew of soldiers—means that you have money, power, and influence. You command respect and have neighborhood cultural cache. It means that you are to be feared and admired in equal measure, which is the ultimate assurance that people will get their just desserts if they work with or against you. What superheroes are to me, wiseguys are to my father. They are protectors and practioners of justice. They wear tailored suits and wingtip shoes instead of a red cape and boots.

* * *

Many critics and scholars of films and comics consider *Superman* to be the first big-budget superhero film. At first, I watched it for my love of the character. Decades later, this film keeps inspiring me to learn about my ancestry, which has yielded intriguing discoveries about other members of my family, including my mother: her assimilation from being Italian to Italian American to American, and all that she suffered and persisted through in that journey. Of all the books I have read; of all of the instructors I have studied with; of all the movies I have seen, my first screening of *Superman* is perhaps the largest factor in why I became a writer who investigates the immigrant experience from a first-generation Italian American perspective.

There have been several incarnations of the Superman story on the screen since 1978. *Superman* remains my favorite of them, not just for what it means to me personally, but also for proving that comics-based motion pictures can a substantive, as well as a lucrative genre of film. Without its success, acclaimed movies such as *Black Panther, Wonder Woman, Guardians of the Galaxy, The Avengers, The Dark Knight, Iron Man, Hellboy, Spider-Man 2,* and others might have taken longer to be made, if ever.

When my spouse and I drove to the venue where my cousin's wedding reception was being held, I thought about my father. I resolved to hold my tongue and enjoy his company. The thought of having cannoli for dessert made my mouth water. I wondered if the DJ would play any Billy Joel songs. I thought of my mother, her eyes red and puffy as she looked at her hometown for the last time, the majestic Maiella in the clear, Apennine Mountain-lined distance.

Mikey and His Constipated Five

Growing up, Uncle Michael worried me. He often had a furious expression in his blood-shot eyes, which was accentuated by the severe arches in his thick eyebrows. His vocabulary was comprised mainly of grunts and profanity, and he didn't walk, so much as he stomped his way around.

He lived with me, my nuclear family, and my grandparents: my father's parents for four years. His first wife, who I have no memory of, divorced him shortly after he came back from his tour of duty in the Vietnam War. Like many who had served in "The Nam," as my father referred to the Vietnam War, Uncle Michael had a difficult time readjusting to civilian life, which often manifested itself in bouts of rage, insomnia, flashbacks, or breaking down and crying for no apparent reason.

"He's shell shocked," Grandfather Joe explained. "I've seen it before."

Indeed. Grandfather Joe was a veteran of World War Two, having driven a Sherman tank in the Battle of the Bulge and the Normandy invasion, among other military operations. My father tried to enlist in the army to fight in The Nam, but he was "rejected," as he put it, on account of having had Rheumatic fever as a child, so he was declared unfit for military service. "I wanted to go," my father said. "But instead they scooped up my kid brother. All he wanted to do was sing."

Before his service, Uncle Michael had been singing doo-wop music on various New York City street corners and under the Triborough Bridge with friends since his early teens. He had a strong baritone-tenor range, and had hooked up with a group called The Symbols. They developed a local following, which led to them opening for the Isley Brothers and recording a few demos.

Sometime later, most of The Symbols went off to fight in The Nam, including Uncle Michael. They never sang together again.

Grandfather Joe had tapes of some of their concerts, and played them once in a while, often after spinning vinyl or playing 8-track tapes of bands and performers from virtually every genre of popular music, most notably the studio albums of The Rascals.

My bedroom was directly above Grandfather Joe's and Grandmother Mary's dining room, which also served as a downsized radio station DJ booth. The table was often cluttered with albums, ashtrays with smoldering cigar embers, album jackets, and stacks of 8-track tapes and cases. His hi-fi system took up an entire wall, and had enormous speakers. Grandmother Mary called them the Twin Towers, which were separated by a complex 8-track player and system of knobs and flashing lights, all of which was capped off by a turntable with a plastic cover. Between Uncle Michael's fondness for singing and my father's musical tastes, some of which matched Grandfather Joe's, ours was a home that was awash in music, which lulled me to sleep and woke me up on several occasions, most often in the forms of birds chirping and Gene Cornish's expressive harmonica in the Rascals' song Groovin.

*   *   *

The only piece of audio equipment that Grandfather Joe enjoyed more than his hi-fi system was his tape recorder and microphone. He would say a few phrases, like "Testing. Testing," or his favorite variant, "Testing, testing, testing, one two, three, try not to pee," and play it back to be sure that his recorder was working as it was supposed to. Then he would speak into the recorder as long as it would let him: the "click" of the "Record" button, informed him that it was a wrap.

Grandfather Joe took particular pleasure in plugging in his microphone and holding it up to someone's mouth while he was taping, regardless of whether or not that person talked. Anyone was fair game, but Uncle Michael was Grandfather Joe's most frequent victim.

As accurate it is to say that my father, Grandfather Joe, and Uncle Michael all enjoyed music, it would also be accurate to say that they also liked to laugh and crack jokes. Those jokes were often at each other's expense, which resulted in Uncle Michael losing his temper more often than not.

"Hey, Mike," Grandfather Joe would say. "Speak in the mike."

"Stop it, Pop."

"Hey Mike, speak in the mike."

"Stop it, Pop."

"Hey Mike, speak—"

"Will you get that thing out of my face?"

"Hey Mike, how's your group? Sing us a song. How about, 'More, More, More?' Or better yet, one that *you* wrote."

"Stop it, Pop."

"You heard it here, folks. I'm talking with Mike—"

"Stop it, Pop."

"Mike Nicoletti, lead singer of Mikey and his Constipated Five."

"Son of a bitch! That does it!"

Then Grandfather Joe would press the stop button. Uncle Michael would become incensed, which resulted in him punching a wall or kicking a chair. Then Grandfather Joe would rewind, then play the tape and burst out laughing. Better infuriation through modern technology.

Interactions like these were the norm in my childhood home life. It was akin to being a cast member of a peculiar and cruel TV sitcom: The Sadistics.

One episode stands out. Grandfather Joe and Uncle Michael had their normal ball-breaking routine, but it escalated faster. Uncle Michael snapped a vinyl record of Johnny Mathis' *Wonderful Wonderful* in half.

Grandfather Joe didn't laugh this time. But Grandmother Mary, who usually kept out of the fray, provided the twist to this episode. She calmly picked up both pieces of *Wonderful Wonderful* placed them on Grandfather Joe's hi-fi.

"I never wanted you, Michael," she said. "I already had my boy, and it ain't you."

A vein bulged from Uncle Michael's forehead. Then he went into the kitchen, grabbed a knife, and threw it at the wall behind my grandparents' heads.

As I consider this now, seeing the knife blade stuck in the wall, its handle shaking, like Uncle Michael's hands, was perhaps his most articulate expression of his experience in The Nam. I can only imagine how frustrated he must have felt to engage in such a course of action in order to make his point to his parents. As someone who was already dealing with being estranged from his spouse, and attempting to recover from Post-Traumatic Stress Disorder, their relentless needling must have felt as if an entire salt factory was poured on Uncle Michael's tormented soul.

Uncle Michael stormed out of the house. The scuffed, white metal door was nudged by a breeze.

"Let's go upstairs, Joefish," my father said to me.

"I've got plenty of other records," Grandfather Joe said. "Hand me the one on top of the speaker, Mary."

Grandmother Mary grabbed a copy of the Rascals' *Groovin.* "You want me to put it on the turntable?"

Grandfather Joe nodded his head. The album's title track warbled from the speakers.

*   *   *

When Grandfather Joe died, Uncle Michael received his entire record and cassette collection. I don't know if Uncle Michael ever purchased another copy of *Wonderful Wonderful,* but I remember him tearing up one Christmas Eve dinner at my sister's house a few years ago, when Johnny Mathis' rendition of "Winter Wonderland" played on her stereo.

Although Uncle Michael had occasional shortness of breath, his spirits were high. He ate linguini, clams, and mussels with gusto. "I'm not supposed to eat shellfish," he said. "I'm allergic to them, but I'm gonna' eat them anyway. Mussels make me horny. Somebody get a mop!"

After dinner, Uncle Michael leaned back on my sister's sofa and yawned the frost off her living room windows. His eyes grew heavy as we listened to the song Groovin, gentle and clear on my sister's stereo;

its bass line, its conga, its tumbadora beat, paving the way for Felix Cavaliere to sing of an idyllic Sunday afternoon, with an expressive harmonica in tow.

Gonna Cry Now

There is no frustration like a dissatisfying ending to a movie with an Italian American protagonist.

Such was the case for my Grandfather Joe and my father, with whom I saw the first *Rocky* when I was a child. We sat in the front row of a movie theater that was somewhere in Long Island, and I remember having terrible pains in my neck from looking straight up at the screen, my ears ringing with Bill Conti's heroic score. Gonna Fly Now.

Seeing *Rocky* was also memorable because it is the first movie that I saw in a theatre without my sister or mother. Prior to *Rocky*, I had seen *The Big Bus* and Dino De Laurentis' remake of *King Kong* in their first theatrical runs, as well as older movies on TV, on such programs and networks as The Late Show, Channel 13, my then-local PBS station, or as was most often the case, on *The Million Dollar Movie*, a nightly series than ran on WOR-TV—Channel 9—in the New York/New Jersey area in the 1960's and 1970's. They played critically acclaimed and box-office hits from the past, most of which I remember were in black and white and starred Humphrey Bogart. Play it, Sam.

My parents claim that the first film I ever saw during its initial theatrical run was *The Godfather*. I neither agree nor disagree. Seeing as how it was released in 1972, when I would have been an infant, there is no way I can recall doing so, no matter how many times I have seen it since or how often I use the dialogue in my everyday speech. Leave the gun. Take the cannolis.

Regardless, seeing *Rocky* is one of my most memorable movie-theatre experiences, in large part due to Grandfather Joe's reaction to the ending, when Apollo Creed wins his boxing match over the underdog unknown club fighter from South Philadelphia, Rocky Balboa, and retains his title as the Heavyweight Champion of the World in a spilt decision. When Apollo, bruised and sweaty, raised his arms in victory, Grandfather Joe was outraged. He did not agree with the movie's turn of events.

"Son of a bitch! They screwed the Italians again," he shouted, as he threw a half-full paper bucket of popcorn and large soda at the screen.

Some people in the audience cheered and applauded Grandfather Joe's actions. Others responded by throwing their food at the screen. My father glared at the screen and then at Grandfather Joe. It was all I could do not to burst out laughing as I watched Milk Duds and Peanut M&Ms pelt Rocky's swollen face and the back of Adrian's head as the movie ended.

Although I was surprised that Rocky did not win the fight, I was puzzled by the issue my father seemed to have with Grandfather Joe. Throughout the movie, and particularly during the heavyweight match where Rocky and Apollo both beat the ever-loving shit out of each other, my father had jumped up out of his seat more than once, yelling, "Go Rocky, go! Kill that Jerkwater," his knuckles slick with popcorn butter. I had never heard the term "Jerkwater" before, but judging by the confused look in Grandfather Joe's eyes, I got the distinct impression that Jerkwater-dom was not quite as derisive or profane as "son of a bitch."

I knew from watching and listening to my parents fight that being referred to as a "Son of a bitch," or worse, "bitch," was not intended as a compliment. I further knew that my Uncle Michael's utterance of the phrase was his way of saying that he had enough of Grandfather Joe laughing or attempting to get laughs at his expense. Not that it mattered. The more exasperated Uncle Michael became, the louder and longer Grandfather Joe laughed.

Any use of profanity was taboo on my part. I learned first-hand, as in the back of father's left and right ones a year or so earlier, when I said "Oh shit," after I knocked my Iron Man action figure off of a shelf in my bedroom and into a trash can. My father slapped me twice: once on each side of my head, telling me that he would "kick my fucking ass" if I ever swore again, "God dammit."

When we drove home from the movie, Grandfather Joe and my father talked about *Rocky*. I don't recall exactly what they said, save one sentence, which was spoken by Grandfather Joe: "Acting is a family business."

The rest of the conversation eludes me, but I have come to learn that Grandfather Joe was making the point that a considerable number of successful film actors are legacies, performers whose parents, and in some cases, grandparents, made their fame and fortune in the entertainment industry. The first examples I learned about were Lon Chaney Jr., and Sr., who, as it was explained to me, had established themselves as "bona fide" movie stars with their respective turns in *The Wolf Man* (in 1941) and *The Phantom of the Opera* (in 1925), the former of which I first saw on The Million Dollar Movie. The second case in point was the Fonda family: Henry and his children Peter and Jane. The men of my family had an immense hatred for Jane, who, aside from having committed the crime of having been born into a life of wealth and privilege, she "flaunted it," as my father once explained to me. In his case, his dislike of Jane was exemplified by her protests of the Vietnam War. He found it convenient, seeing as how her family's prestige and affluence had assured she would never have to participate in it in any capacity, much less in actual combat. Given that Uncle Michael was wounded in his tour of duty in "The Nam," and that Grandfather Joe was a veteran of World War Two, they felt that her activism derived more from an offensive sense of entitlement than it was of a genuine concern and campaign for peace in the world. Seeing the infamous photograph of her sitting on a North Vietnamese anti-aircraft gun enraged them, just as it did other Americans, which resulted in her being nicknamed "Hanoi Jane." For the men of my family, Jane's actions insulted the people who were risking and sacrificing their well-being for the American way of life that made her charmed existence possible, which was to say that she slighted Uncle Michael: they took Jane's actions personally. In their point of view, she was the poster child for all that they felt was unscrupulous about the entertainment industry, whose most powerful people gave faces and names to some of the members of the American elite. That Jane Fonda was as talented an actor as her father Henry and achieved fame and fortune on her own merits and skills was irrelevant. The men of my family viewed her as a spoiled brat who was spending her father's money in ways that antagonized working class people and dismissed blue-collar values, which pertained to most Italian Americans; people on both sides of my family. To them, Jane's existence and behavior on and off the silver screen represented how the elite exploited and disregarded the labors of the people who did the working, living, and dying, both in, and far away from America, and how unlikely they were to achieve a similar status, in spite of their efforts.

When *Rocky* was a success, having had ten academy award nominations and winning three of them for Best Picture, Best Director, and Best Film Editing, the adults of my family were ecstatic, particularly the men, even before any of them saw the film. Rocky's victories with the academy, with a venerated established order, had solidified what *The Godfather* had started, in terms of respect for the skills and contributions of people of Italian descent in another stratum of American culture. Even though the 1970's had an opulence of brilliant performances of Italian-American artists on and off the screen, such as Al Pacino in *The Godfather, The Godfather Part Two, Serpico,* and *Dog Day Afternoon,* Francis Ford Coppola's script for *Patton,* his production of *THX 1138, The Conversation, American Graffiti,* and *Apocalypse Now,* his direction of *The Godfather, The Godfather Part Two, and Apocalypse Now,* Robert DeNiro in the Martin Scorsese-directed *Mean Streets* and his Oscar winning turn in *The Godfather Part Two,* John Cazale in both *Godfather* films, *Dog Day Afternoon* and *The Conversation,* among other artists and films—Sylvester Stallone represented what my family prided themselves on: persistence, diligence, gaining prosperity and respect by earning your keep. My Grandfather Joe was the youngest of 10 siblings, most of whom were born in Napoli, Italia. Having grown up in abject poverty in the Canarsie neighborhood of Brooklyn, New York City, Grandfather Joe had to drop out of school in the eighth grade to help support his family. He worked for many years as an ice carrier, endured the Great Depression, and then enlisted in the United States Army days after the bombing of Pearl Harbor. He went to work for the Metropolitan Transit Authority soon after he came home from Europe, as did Uncle Michael when he came home from Vietnam.

To my family, Sylvester Stallone, who also wrote the screenplay for Rocky—after seeing Chuck Wepner, "The Bayonne Bleeder" knock down Muhammad Ali in a title defense fight in Cleveland, Ohio's Richfield Coliseum in the ninth round—was one of them, not just because of their shared ethnicity. Their love for him also lied in his belief in himself and dogged determination. He refused to sell the script for *Rocky* to a studio unless he played the leading role. The Bayonne Bleeder went the distance, only to lose the match in a split decision, just as Rocky did. Gonna cry now.

As much as my family enjoyed the first two *Godfather* films, the first *Rocky* film made their hearts swell with unadulterated Italian American masculine pride. Seeing Rocky hitting raw meat in training and go the distance against a superior opponent were metaphors for how they felt: determined, strong, and woefully underestimated; more powerful than people might have otherwise thought. The character of Rocky Balboa was a blue-collar man: he worked as a collector for a loan shark, and fought in clubs, for which he never received a large payday. Rocky struggled to make ends meet, just as they did. Add to the fact that he had turtles named "Cuff" and "Link," a goldfish named "Moby Dick," and loved them as much as his girlfriend Adrian and her older brother and his best friend Paulie. Such details showed a humane side to an otherwise rough and tumble character. They saw themselves in Sylvester Stallone's interpretation of Rocky Balboa more than they ever did in Al Pacino's takes on the characters Michael Corleone, Sonny Wortzik, or Frank Serpico. Rocky was set in the present day. *The Godfather*, *Serpico*, and *Dog Day Afternoon* were in the past. *The Godfather* was a work of fiction. *Serpico* was based on Peter Mass's eponymously named biography and *Dog Day Afternoon* was based on "The Boys in the Bank," an article that was published in *Time* magazine in 1972. No Wyoming. That's not a country.

As entertaining as these films—these adaptations of texts were to my family—their effectiveness was more to do with artifice than realism. If acting was a family business, Sylvester Stallone's screenplay and performance of Rocky Balboa punched the door to the estates of the elite down; it resonated with audience members who saw themselves as the underdog, with those who had no connections. *The Godfather* is a film about the Corleones, an Italian American crime family. Connections are a defining characteristic of any family, whether they are law-abiding citizens or work in organized crime. Rocky's group of people is compiled of friends from his South Philadelphia neighborhood. His parents are referred to in the movie but are never seen. Unlike *The Godfather*, Rocky Balboa's existence is not dependent of family ties in the traditional Italian-American sense. Rocky's interactions with his friends provides a fascinating take on the notion that family does not end with blood, whereas in *The Godfather* films, members of The Corleone family drop left and right, sometimes at the hand of their own kin. You broke my heart Fredo.

Before Sylvester Stallone achieved Hollywood stardom, he once slept at the New York Port Authority bus terminal for three weeks; he toiled through Hollywood with cameo appearances, uncredited roles, and even a porno flick, *The Party at Kitty and Studs,* which was renamed *Italian Stallion* after the success of *Rocky*. Sylvester Stallone knows what it is like to be broke; he understands disappointment, rejection, and hunger. Perhaps most notably, he also seems to possess an almost insatiable drive to be successful in his chosen field, in spite of the great odds against him: like an unknown boxer who is offered a shot at the World Heavyweight Championship Title. When the character Rocky Balboa lost the fight on a technicality, my father felt as if he lost. Grandfather Joe felt as if Italian Americans were cheated out of a victory they had fought long and hard for and earned the right to achieve. God dammit.

Biggs' Deal

The years 1977 and 1978 overflowed with *Star Wars*. I screened it for the first four times in my life those years, in the times before my family had cable television; long before streaming existed, the last of which was in a drive-in theatre screen near Lake George, New York. My father took me to see it. Our view was from a rock that was on the precipice of the campgrounds my family and I stayed at for the only family vacation we ever took by ourselves. This was also the first time that I saw it in an open-air theatre.

My father laughed and smoked Benson and Hedges cigarettes throughout the movie. We heard some of *Star Wars'* sounds and dialogue from the nearest speakers, which sprang from the gravel like metallic sunflowers. My joy whooshed, hummed, and beeped from the sunflowers. I stuffed my face with boxes of Raisinets and long, loud slurps of root beer.

It was clear and cool outside, about 60 degrees or so, and the stars above the screen were as bright as the ones on it. The screen itself seemed more like a part of the upstate New York sky than an enormous aluminum rectangle below it. *This is the best,* I thought to myself. *A movie about space in the widest, the most open space I have ever been in. Wow.*

For all of *Star Wars'* splendors; for all of its wondrous places: Tatooine, Mos Eisley Spaceport; the Death Star; for all of its marvelous vehicles—Star Destroyers, Luke's Land Speeder, the Millennium Falcon, Tie Fighters, X-Wing Fighters; the protagonists and antagonists who populate its plot, my main attraction to *Star Wars* is its minor characters. They have the greatest allure for me, which I first noticed when I saw it with my father in upstate New York.

A notable example is the character Biggs Darklighter. He and Luke were best friends growing up on the planet Tatooine. Garrick Hagon portrayed him in *Star Wars*, and his backstory was covered more extensively in both the *Star Wars Storybook* and Marvel Comics 6-issue adaptation of the film. I read these after my first *Star Wars* screening.

In these iterations, Biggs is introduced to the audience wearing an empire uniform with a black cape. He returns to Tatooine to let Luke know that he plans to leave the empire and join the rebellion. He tells Luke this in case he doesn't return, and because he wants him to know that he's fighting "on the side I believe in."

Luke, who is itching to leave Tatooine and find excitement elsewhere, says that the Empire wouldn't be interested in their home world. Biggs retorts with "Things always change."

None of these lines made it to the final cut of *Star Wars*. While Biggs is referred to early in the movie, his first onscreen appearance is when he and Luke meet in the Rebel fleet hangar. Before Luke met Ben Kenobi, Han Solo, Chewbacca: Chewie, or Princess Leia, Biggs is the character who gives Luke a perspective that goes beyond the two-suns he stares at during every Tatooine dusk; that there is more going around and beyond him besides his work on his Uncle Owen and Aunt Beru's Moisture Farm.

When I saw Biggs on the screen, I clapped. My father furrowed his eyebrows.

"What the shit, Joefish? It's not like Al Pacino's on the screen."

"That's Biggs Darklighter," I said. "He's great!"

"Biggs?!?! Biggs deal. What's so great about him?"

"Biggs and Luke are best friends," I said. "Like you and Uncle Steve."

Uncle Steve was not a blood relative. He and my father had been tight since their teenage years, when they met in a schoolyard brawl. As my father tells it, they came to the aid of a mutual friend and things grew from there. Uncle Steve had, if you will pardon the pun, dark hair and a dashing moustache, just like Biggs. The more images of Biggs I saw, the more convinced I was of his resemblance to my not-uncle.

Biggs' call sign was Red Three. Luke's was Red Five. Another pilot, Red Two—who was also a minor character—was Wedge Antilles. I had learned that Wedge was regarded as one of the best pilots in the Rebel fleet from other *Star Wars* themed novels and stories. Denis Lawson portrayed him. Denis is also the uncle of Ewan McGregor, who went on to play Ben Kenobi in the *Star Wars* prequel films and the Obi-Wan Kenobi Disney series. Ewan was my age when *Star Wars* was released, which is one of the reasons why I am a fan of his work. Like me, Ewan is also a child of the 1970's: a fellow Generation X'er. Unlike me, Ewan is related to a professional actor who achieved international fame and admiration by playing an ace fighter pilot, a so-called minor character, and one who has become one of the finest performing artists of our peer group.

As the Battle of Yavin was fought, the X-Wing fleet was reduced to three pilots, all of whom were from Red Squadron: Luke, Biggs, and Wedge. Darth Vader eventually joins the battle in his custom Tie Fighter, flanked by two other Tie Fighters. They damage Wedge's X-Wing, and he withdraws from the battle. Then Darth Vader and his wingmen speed through the Death Star trench. Biggs tries to cover Luke, but Darth Vader fires at Biggs' X-Wing.

Biggs yells, "Wait!" His ship then explodes, and flashes of its fiery debris fade.

I tear up when I see the scene now just as I did when I saw it in Lake George. Part of it is because of my familiarity with Biggs, having read written and illustrated versions with more developed versions of him. It is also due to seeing Uncle Steve in Biggs's face. He died a few years back of stomach cancer. My father doesn't like to speak about it.

Another reason why I cry is because of my friend Phil, who was my original best friend. We met in nursery school. We went trick-or-treating together. We played on the same Soccer team. I went to my first sleepover at his family's house. We both lived with our grandparents. My Grandmother Mary and his Grandmother Winnie were also close friends. Phil and I played with each other's superhero and Star Wars action figures; we traded football, baseball, and Star Wars trading cards. We were our own Red Squadron.

He moved to Massachusetts two years after my Lake George screening. His father got a promotion at work. I was happy for Phil's father, but I cried every day for two weeks.

Grandmother Mary was also despondent. She and Winnie never saw each other again.

Even though Phil and I wrote letters and had the occasional long-distance phone call—back in the days when most households had landlines and making long distance calls was a rare treat for me—we eventually lost touch. While such a development is not uncommon among friends whose families relocate, especially at young ages, dealing with the reality of not seeing or hearing someone important in my life for the foreseeable future, if not forever, was jarring. My world was annihilated, like the Death Star.

Since that time, I have discovered that Phil is to me what Biggs is to Luke: my first taste of the bittersweet flavor of growing up, which resonates for me more and more when I ponder Biggs edited dialogue: things always change.

Part of my sadness at Biggs' death is also to do with seeing it on a screen that was larger than any of the others I had viewed *Star Wars* on before. The drive-in screen's massive size made the film seem more mythopoeic than it already was to me, and especially the scenes I liked or was most moved by. Seeing was everything for me back then.

The full title of the movie is *Star Wars: Episode IV, A New Hope*. The "Episode IV" part indicated that more of the saga had already been written, even if only George Lucas knew about it. The drive-in screen made me want to look closer into every aspect of the *Star Wars* saga.

When Luke destroyed the Death Star, people clapped, cheered, and honked their horns in the parking lot. My father and I joined them, my fingers sticky with Raisinet chocolate.

Even so, as was the case in my previous screenings of *Star Wars*, I was outraged on Chewie's behalf. I asked my father why he didn't get an award of any kind, having helped Luke stick it to the Empire.

"F-heck if I know, Joefish. Why didn't Al Pacino get an Oscar for *The Godfather*? *Serpico*? *Dog Day Afternoon*? Sometimes people get overlooked for no good reason. Capisce?"

I sipped my root beer, and my father lit a new smoke. We watched the credits roll, my thoughts swept away by John Williams' music, the revving of engines; station wagon doors slamming shut; the flashing chests of fireflies, side by side with mosquitoes in the tall grass beside the rock.

This Means Something

I didn't know much about Indiana. My first screening of *Close Encounters of the First Kind* felt like I was watching home movies, even though no one in my nuclear family was a native of the American Midwest.

When the Neary family makes its first appearance in *Close Encounters,* the audience sees them in their tract house, which is cluttered. The most prominent feature is a train board populated by bridges, train engines and boxcars, trees, switches, and newspaper pages. One of the pages covers a ceramic figure of the Walt Disney incarnation of the Carlo Collodi created-character Pinocchio, which plays the song "When You Wish Upon a Star' as it rotates. The family also argues whether or not they should go out miniature golfing or see the film *Pinocchio*, which is playing at a movie theatre. Roy is favor of the latter, but the rest of the Nearys choose golf. My childhood home looked and sounded exactly like this: cluttered, energetic, and blaring, which led my mother to refer to our family as "The LOUD Family."

Seeing Roy's train board makes me think of my father, who also collects trains. In addition to displaying some of his favorite Lionel toy engines in various rooms of his condominium, there is a train board that takes up an entire room. I don't think that I have ever seen him happier than he is when he sets up: he "reconfigures" his board, run his favorite engines, or talk about them when he has company.

My father's trains are my long boxes of comic books. Most of them are in my home office closet. Others are stacked against the wall, which makes our cat Max happy, since it gives him a high tower to perch on. He did not come from my spouse's womb, but he takes after me, and as we and our comics age, an inescapable truth becomes clearer and clearer: I am my father's son in more than name. To say that my father and I are passionate human beings is tantamount to saying that Steven Spielberg is one of cinema's most acclaimed producers and filmmakers.

I also have a *Close Encounters* movie poster in my home office. When I look at it, my eyes go to the road that leads to a cloud of light in the distance. Its source is beyond what the eye can see, a visual riddle, triggered by the categories of "close encounters," whose lexicon was established by UFO-ologist J. Allen Hynek. The first kind refers to the sighting of a UFO. The second refers to physical evidence. The third is contact. These classifications are placed directly above the light, which invites the viewer to take a closer look at it, to wonder who or what kind of sentient beings are behind it.

This in turn makes me recall the moving performances of Carey Guffey as Barry Guiler and Melinda Dillon as Jillian Guiler, his mother. The scene where the aliens kidnap Barry from his and Jillian's Muncie, Indiana house stands out. Jillian sees a spacecraft emerge from a cloud as she takes out the garbage. She calmly walks inside her house, locks the doors and windows, and closes the chimney chute as the aliens attempt to enter it. Vibrant shades of red, yellow, orange, and green light pour through the house as the UFO land, which has caused the Guiler's dishwasher to spit out water, dishes, and utensils, the vacuum cleaner to start running through the kitchen, and Johnny Mathis's song "Chances Are" plays on a turntable. While Barry is drawn to it, Jillian is frightened and repelled, which causes her to shout, "Go away!"

Nevertheless, Barry goes to a dog door, and crawls through it. Jillian grabs his legs, but the aliens take him, and the ship vanishes. Jillian screams Barry's name and runs after the UFO, storm clouds dissipating in the Indiana sky.

As much my heart always goes out to Jillian, I still identify most with Barry: being close to the character's age when I first saw *Close Encounters,* I looked at the aliens and their marvelous ships from his perspective. I found myself wanting to go to the light; I wanted to go for a ride in space with the aliens, just so I could have a respite from the LOUD family. The thought of hanging out with beings from somewhere other than New York with whips like the ones in the film thrilled me. Jillian seemed like a caring, responsible, and dedicated single parent, but I admired Barry's fearless and trusting nature; his curiosity and enthusiasm for making new friends and going somewhere that he had never been to before.

As I consider this further, taking a ride with the aliens also appealed to my desire to escape my family situation. My parents' tempers seemed to be getting shorter as I got older. Their incessant bickering had escalated into shoving and throwing plates at each other. I remember my mother taking lots of pills, before and after they fought, with money and taxes being the main items at issue. Sometimes the fights got so brutal that she took my sister and I to one of her friend's house, where she cursed, cried, and smoked. I saw my mother driving the car in the scene where Ronnie takes the Neary kids to her sister's, after Roy steals chicken wire from a neighbor's yard, takes the trash can from a garbage collector's hands, and throws bricks, plants, and shovels dirt into his family's kitchen window and sink. Ronnie had the same disgusted expression on her face that my mother often had when we peeled out of our driveway.

* * *

Seeing the re-release of *Close Encounters in* 2017 was a succulent treat for me. Other than me and my partner, there were only two other people in the theatre. Each frame was as filled with wonderous visual and sonic treats as it was when I first saw it. My eyes widened as I saw Roy's train board, Devil's Tower, the arena, and the Mother ship. The famous five-note sequence that's played throughout the film brought out constellations of goose bumps on my arms and legs.

Then I noticed something about the film that I hadn't before. In the scene where Barry's electronic toys activate themselves, they scatters his spelling and letter blocks across the room. I used to own the blocks and the police car whose siren wailed and woke Jillian up as it rolled into her bedroom. When I first watched this part of the film, I was captivated by Barry's toys moving by themselves instead of the toys themselves.

Decades later, I have begun to understand why Steven Spielberg filled Barry's room with toys that children of 1977 played with. This is the scene that introduces Barry to the audience, which also helped to make me and other people my age see ourselves in the character.

This connection has only grown tighter through the years. Seeing the re-release of *Close Encounters* in a theatre as an adult, I was transported back to my childhood: I felt the plastic of the number 3 block, sticky with Coca-Cola as I stacked it on top of the orange and yellow 2 and 1 blocks on top of the Cherrywood toy chest in my bedroom, scratched, scuffed, and stained with moonlight.

This feeling of intimacy has also made me view *Close Encounters* as a metaphor for my understanding of heritage. Although none of the film's main characters are Italian, I submit that food is used as interestingly in it as it is in *The Godfather*. The main example that comes to my mind is the famous "mashed potatoes scene." Roy Neary, the movie's main character, who is played by Richard Dreyfus, is eating dinner with his family. Roy has seen a UFO, has been fired from his job, and is obsessed by his experience. His wife Ronnie, who is played by Teri Garr, passes him a bowl of mashed potatoes. Roy spoons some onto his plate, and then takes a few more scoops. Once he does so, he spreads some of the potatoes out on his plate and starts carving ridges into the side of the remaining heap. Roy stops only when he feels his family staring at him with baffled and angry looks in their eyes. He breaks down and cries, saying, "I guess you've noticed there's something a little strange with Dad. This means something. This is important."

There were no cannolis to take. No murders. No uncomfortable laughs. Just an ordinary American family caught in the maelstrom of their father's obsession with something extraordinary. As intrigued as I am with *Close Encounters'* sights and sounds, the interactions of the Neary family resonate with me, particularly in how they cope with Roy's struggle in dealing with his sighting. My family often got issues of their chest at the dinner table, which frequently ended in tears, as it did for Roy in this particular scene. His reaction was plausible, and I cried along with him and the rest of his family.

While *Close Encounters* is classified as a Science-Fiction film, I find the human interactions to be the fuel that makes the film's engine go.

Leo Tolstoy's novel *Anna Karenina* begins with the notion that "every unhappy family is unhappy in its own way." My parents' fights usually began as discussions about the LOUD family's financial matters. Coupled with watching baseball games, going to the movies with them provided a reprieve from our home of broken dishes, empty wine bottles, ash trays, and clothes strewn on chairs and tables. Most of the films I remember seeing with my family were in the late 1970's and early 1980's, which were blockbuster films that built on the success of Steven Spielberg's adaptation of Peter Benchley's novel *Jaws* in 1975. By the time I saw *Close Encounters,* George Lucas' space fantasy epic *Star Wars* was out, which was escapist entertainment. I had yet to learn about Watergate, The Vietnam War, or what a mortgage was, but I knew that going to the movies calmed my parents down, even if a film we watched depicted other families in turmoil, such as the Nearys. Watching Roy, Ronnie, and their children shout and cry at each other are some of the first recollections I have in considering that families don't always get along. While my friends told me that their parents fought, I didn't witness it first hand, and I suspected that even if I did, it would not have been with the same virulence and violence my parents brought to theirs.

Roy and Jillian are young parents, almost the same age my parents were at the time of *Close Encounters'* first release. I am not a parent of human children, but seeing a dog in the shadow of light, trotting among all of the other abductees who get off the mother ship in the film's final act remind me of mine and my partner Beth's fur babies: Roxy and Stella Bella, which fills me with equal amounts if joy and sorrow. While I have always been happy to see the people and animals return to their home in the film, I also find myself feeling anxious for them: will they be reunited with their humans? Will the government help them readjust to life on Earth, given the amount of time and changes that have passed and taken place since they were last home? And if so, how?

Steven Spielberg wrote the novelization of the film, which has a scene where Roy writes a letter to his children where he attempts to explain his actions. As interesting as this is from the perspective of revising one of *Close Encounters'* storylines, it's challenging for me to get past the pain Roy has caused to his family in its novelization, as well the film itself, which will continue after he leaves Earth. If I have learned anything since my first screening of *Close Encounters,* it's that the trauma of my parents escalated arguments impacted me in ways that I'm only beginning to understand.

This understanding has come with lots of therapy, which started when I became a spouse. One of the adages that my therapist and I investigated was that "Children learn what they live." Ironically, my mother had a plaque with this statement on it in the kitchen of my childhood home. If this statement is true, then I learned that family tumult was normal, that abuse was as part of my home as a sink or toilet. If only I could wash or flush my trauma and its fallout away.

Fortunately for me, I have an incredible support system. Abuse cycles are curious phenomena, and they are challenging to break, but I have begun to do so. In addition to my therapist, I also have an off-the-charts loving partner in Beth, whose emotional intelligence is as high as her intellect. She also had a tumultuous upbringing. As a result, we decided not to become parents of human children. I did not—and I don't—want to cause anyone any pain, especially the people who I am supposed to nurture.

I couldn't love Stella Bella or Roxy any more than if they came from mine or my Beth's bodies. They help me unlearn; to overcome the challenges of my upbringing. Because of them, my therapist, and my chosen family, it's becoming clear to me: if children learn what they live, adults can unlearn and learn again. Abuse cycles can be broken. Movies can be remastered and give audiences new perspectives about what it means, has meant, or could mean to be a human being in the world, even if they leave it, like Roy, my heart swelling as a traveling city takes to the clear Wyoming sky, my ears awash in triumphant cellos, violins, tubas, and trumpets.

Kentucky Fried Idiot

The Italians always prevail. This was my father's mindset when we saw *Rocky II* with my cousin Domenico: Dom. It was summer. Gypsy moth caterpillars infested our back yard. Empty Piels beer bottles lined the kitchen counter like excommunicated chess pieces, and Benson and Hedges cigarette smoke constantly fogged our mirrored living room wall.

I was excited to see Dom. We usually saw each other two or three times a year when we were boys, which occurred during gatherings on my mother's side of my family, such as wedding receptions, engagements, communion, confirmation, or christening parties. The adults smoked, danced, and drank all kinds of exotic sounding wines, such as Trebbiano and Montepulciano. Dom and I swapped baseball cards, comic books, and asked the bartenders to put as many Maraschino cherries as they could in our glasses of Coca-Cola or 7-Up.

Dom is also fluent in Italian, or at least the Orsognese dialect of it, as is (and was) the rest of my mother's side of the family. Antonio and Lina, Dom's parents, are my *padrini,* my godparents, and I tried to pick up as much Orsognese Italian as I could when I saw them. I can still taste the syrup of the grenadine from all of the cherry cokes and Shirley Temples we guzzled.

My father was also excited to see Dom. Although he got on well with my mother's side of the family, I noticed that he often seemed to be a bit more nervous around them than he usually was around people. Although he had my padrini and just about every other one of my mother's family members laughing as soon as he entered a room, he took quicker drags of his Camel cigarettes. He spoke faster. He always seemed to have a beer in his hand. I am uncertain if this was due to his language skills, or his perceived lack thereof, because the Italian he spoke was pidgin; more Italian American than Italian European.

Perhaps my father's apparent anxiety had to do with his ultra-extroversion; his desire to be loved by everyone, and particularly Antonio, Lina, and company, was such that he always wanted to make a great impression on them, as an American-born and raised man who took pride in his ethnicity. Having not been fluent in any form of Italian, I can only imagine the apprehension he felt when he was in the company of my mother's side of the family. My putative sense of our heritage notwithstanding, my father was more vulnerable than I was capable of fathoming at the time. He still is.

Maybe the Piels kept his concerns in abeyance on this particular day, but the prospect of having Antonio, Lina, and Dom at our house filled him with pride, in the home he worked 60 hours a week to afford and for the chance to play host on his turf, on Long Island, which was to him what New York City was to Lina and Tony: the place they chose to make a life in. Other than having them at our Teed Street digs, he saw taking Dom to see *Rocky II* as an expression of his love of being a Long Island homeowner, Italian, and American.

"We'll have a great time," my father said. "Rocky will win. The Italians always come through."

*   *   *

We saw *Rocky II* at a cineplex in the town of Syosset, which was a fairly short drive from my family's Teed Street digs. The theatre was distinguished for me by having a balcony, which I had never seen in a cineplex before.

We sat in the front row of the balcony's center aisle. I remember watching the crowd gather below. The theatre was packed, and there was a buzz. People wore T-shirts with Sylvester Stallone's face ironed on them. Others had undershirts with "Rocky Balboa Fan Club" and "The Italian Stallion" written on them in black magic marker.

"Look at this," Dom said. "It's like we're at a real fight. Live from Syosset!"

Dom's words were prophetic. I can still see my father, shuffling in his seat, shaking his head as the movie started with footage from the first *Rocky* film, when Apollo Creed is announced the winner of the fight by a split decision and retains his Heavyweight Championship belt.

For all of the film's buildup, I remember being pleasantly surprised at the number of times I laughed out loud. There were lots of jokes in the film, such as, "You want to have a good time? Then you need a good watch!"

Of all of *Rocky II's* comedic moments, I had the biggest laugh when Mickey, Rocky's manager, tries to increase Rocky's speed by making him chase a chicken. Rocky voices his objections, saying that it's "embarrassing" and "not very mature," but to no avail. The chicken evades Rocky's grasp, despite his best efforts, which causes him to stop running after it. Mickey asks him what's wrong. Rocky replies, "I feel like a Kentucky Fried Idiot."

Dom and I laughed our faces off. My father smiled, and took a long, satisfied drag of his Camel smoke.

* * *

For those who don't know: *Rocky* movies cannot exist without melodrama to balance out their moments of levity, and *Rocky II* is opulent with both. Apollo challenges Rocky to a rematch. Rocky decides to retire from boxing because of the damage he has received to his right eye. His wife Adrian becomes pregnant. Rocky tries to make commercials but fails because of his poor reading skills. He gets a job working at his friend Paulie's slaughterhouse, but gets laid off due to cutbacks. Rocky talks with Butkus, his English mastiff, as he bathes him. Adrian gets her old pet shop job back. Rocky decides to accept Apollo's rematch challenge. Adrian objects. His training goes poorly, knowing Adrian's misgivings. Paulie notices this and excoriates Adrian at the pet shop. Adrian's water breaks. She gives birth to a boy and slips into a coma. Rocky becomes distraught. He prays in the hospital's chapel. Mickey joins him.

Rocky reads parts of Edgar Rice Burroughs' novel *The Deputy Sherriff of Comanche County*.

Rocky also reads a poem to Adrian, one that he wrote himself, which references their first date, which took place in the first *Rocky* film. The poem begins:

> Remember when we was on ice skates
> and I thought that you were supposed to be great
> so I kept giving you lip
> and you kept trying to slip
> so I could catch you.

I remember hearing people behind us sniff. I was surprised. For a film that many—myself included—had anticipated as a 2-hour boxing match, it seemed to be more of a soap opera hoagie, with the boxing matches as loaves of semolina bread made by United Artists.

When Adrian woke up, she and Rocky saw their child: Rocky Junior, for the first time. The she told Rocky to "win."

Rocky trained hard. The opening notes of Bill Conti's iconic song "Gonna Fly Now" played loud and clear in Dolby Stereo. The speakers shook as the updated, lighter version of the song boomed, as children ran with Rocky to the top step of the Philadelphia Art Institute, chanting his name. The crowd joined in, myself and Dom included.

"Madone," my father said. "Let's see some boxing now!"

*   *   *

People hollered and shouted as *Rocky II's* fight scene started. From our vantage point, it felt as if we were in the nose bleed seats of the Philadelphia Spectrum, watching Apollo and Rocky taunt and knock each other's teeth down their throats. The match was dubbed "Superfight II," and it had all of the visual and emotional trimmings of a *Rocky* fight.

The picture was blurry and moved in slow motion in Superfight II's definitive moments: when Apollo hit Rocky hard in his right eye; when Rocky landed his first body blow to Apollo's ribs; and when both fighters hit the ground in the 15th round.

It all came down to who got up first. People were standing in their seats behind us, as well as below. The majority of the theatre audience implored Rocky to stand up and shout at the screen, including my father.

"C'mon, Rocco! Punch like an Italian!"

Bill Conti's brass section conjured the days of the Rome Coliseum in its heyday. Some people averted their eyes as Rocky staggered to his feet. Dom and I slurped our sodas with anticipation.

The big finish saw Apollo almost on his feet, only to slide to the canvas at the last second. Rocky climbed the ring's ropes and stood up. The referee declared Apollo "out." Ladies and gentlemen, meet your new fictitious heavyweight champion of the world, Philadelphia's finest: The Italian Stallion, Rocky Balboa.

"The Italian guy won! The Italian guy won! I knew he would," my father yelled.

Dom and I high-fived each other. My father lit a new Benson and Hedges and took a long, satisfied drag. An updated, disco-beat version of the original *Rocky* theme played as the credits rolled down the screen in gold letters against a black background, which were the same colors as Rocky's boxing trunks. It buzzed, popped and grooved with assurance that Rocky was not only the best in the world at what he did, he had also earned it, one choreographed left hook at a time, a smile plastered on my father's bearded, sweaty American Italian face.

The Bronze Age

Not all Batmans are created equal. With all due respect to Michael Keaton, Christian Bale, and all of the other actors who have portrayed The Dark Knight, Adam West is my Batman. Given the long hours my parents spent at work during my childhood, there was a time in my life when I saw West's face at least as much as my mother's or father's face, if not more so. My introduction to his take on the character coincided with the first time my mother had a job in her married life. In addition to assuring that bills were paid in full and on time, they tried to save enough money to afford a bigger house in a more upscale neighborhood, which they described as "living closer to the water," the fact that we lived on an island notwithstanding. West's three-season TV show tenure as Batman/Bruce Wayne may have begun and ended in the late 1960's, but seeing reruns of *Batman* made my late 1970's childhood less lonely and considerably more bearable.

Of all of the pleasures I got from watching *Batman,* I often did so with my grandmother Mary, which made my viewing of the show all the more joyous. Her enthusiasm for the show was palpable. It felt like Super Bowl Sunday five days a week, where Jif peanut butter was as essential to the experience as West's Batman or Burt Ward's Robin. Not only did Grandmother Mary consume copious amounts of Jif with me, we ate gobs of it with spoons in our own personal jars. That she allowed me to do so was a joy. That she enjoyed the way we ate peanut butter was wonderful. My munching and slurping of chocolate milk augmented the visual onomatopoeia title cards of the words Bam! Krunch! Ka-Pow! that flashed across the screen in canary yellow, emerald-green, sky blue, and rocket red colored lettering during the fight scenes of each episode.

Grandmother Mary and I enjoyed all of the villains in Batman's rogue's gallery, but our favorites were Penguin and Catwoman. Penguin was played by Burgess Meredith. I knew him from the movie *Rocky*. He played Mickey Goldmill, Rocky Balboa's trainer. She knew him from a TV show called *The Twilight Zone*. I had never seen an episode of it.

"It's a good show," Grandmother Mary said. "They tell great stories."

Multiple actresses played Catwoman. My favorite was Eartha Kitt. I liked the way she rolled her r's. Her smile was killer, and the Catwoman costume complimented her shapely figure. Purr-fect!

"She's a great singer too," grandmother Mary said. "I think your father has one of her records."

I also liked that some villains were created specifically for the show, such as Egghead. He had a bald head and was played by Vincent Price. Grandmother Mary mentioned that she and my grandfather Joe saw him in a lot of horror films in the 1930's and 1940's. He had also been a radio actor, which Grandmother Mary told me was "her version of TV" when she was "a young lady." Egg-cellent.

The one rule Grandmother Mary had for me was to be sure that my feet were covered at all times. She believed that bare feet made me vulnerable to catching a cold, or worse, getting sick. My father had rheumatic fever as a child. As Grandmother Mary explained, it kept him in bed for a long time, and she never wanted to see anyone else be that sick again if they could avoid it. To her way of thinking, covering my feet was an easy, yet effective preventative measure for doing this. I'm still not clear if she had any reputable scientific data or evidence that informed her way of thinking, but I knew that being barefoot around her was not an option.

There were times I forgot. When my feet weren't covered with socks, slippers, or any other kind of footwear, she reminded me of her rule by using the following phrase: "Put shoes on!"

Grandmother Mary also used this phrase as a way of telling me to take care of myself.

For instance, my mother came home from work early one day. I wore a pair of socks. My mother saw me eating Jif on a spoon, which infuriated her. I knew this because she had a tendency to move her eyebrows metronomically when she expressed her displeasure with something I did; they moved in sync with each word she said, and this particular instance was a memorable case in point.

"Jo. Seph. What. Is. This?"

"It's Jif peanut butter, Mama. Extra crunchy. You want some?"

"No. I. Don't. Thank. You."

"Oh sure. You mind if I finish?"

"Let the boy enjoy his snack, Marie," Grandmother Mary said. "Lighten up."

Then my mother glared at me and took a deep breath.

"Jo. Seph. Get. Up. Stairs. Right. Now!"

I handed the spoon to Grandmother Mary, who looked me straight in the eyes.

"Joseph. Put shoes on." she said.

I nodded, then ran upstairs into my room. I could hear Grandmother Mary and my mother shouting at each other as if they were beside me. I stubbed my toe. Oooff!

* * *

One day, *Batman the Movie* was on instead of the TV show reruns. Burgess Meredith portrayed Penguin. Lee Merriweather played Catwoman. The Riddler and Joker were in it, and they were played by Frank Gorshin and Caesar Romero, respectively. Grandmother Mary watched and laughed as Batman and Robin thwarted their rogues gallery from taking over the world. I remember that her biggest laughs came when the Joker was on the screen.

"Look at that," she said. "His face is painted white, but I can still see Caesar Romero's moustache. Holy bad makeup!"

West's flippant take on Batman had me in stitches for the entire movie. This was especially the case in the scene where Batman runs all over a dock on the Gotham City waterfront, trying to dispose of an activated bomb. Every time he thinks he has a clear spot to dispose of it, people or animals show up. Concerned about saving everyone, and somewhat frustrated, Batman said my all-time favorite movie line:

"Some days you just can't get rid of a bomb!"

"You got that right," Grandmother Mary said, as she lit a cigarette. Our bursts of laughter splashed in water on the dock. Ka-Boom!

I got up to use the bathroom. My socks were on the arm rests of her navy blue and hot pink floral-patterned couch. Grandmother Mary cleared her throat.

"Joseph! Put shoes on!"

* * *

Within a month after watching *Batman the Movie*, I had enough comics to fill two milk crates. Grandmother Mary gave me the crates, and read the books with me. She enjoyed any script or plot that involved the Penguin. As Burgess Meredith stated, "Great quivering jellyfish!"

The best part about coming of age as a comic book reader when I did, which comic historians refer to as The Bronze Age, which in comics parlance refers to the time period of 1970 to 1985, when many new superhero comic book characters were introduced or established characters had their own series. Some of them didn't last very long, such as Marvel Comics' *The Man Called Nova*, which chronicled the adventures of Richard Ryder, a Queens-born teenager, much like the Marvel Comics character Peter Parker/Spider Man, who is given super-powers by an alien much like the DC Comics character Hal Jordan/ Green Lantern. *Nova* was cancelled after 25 issues, even though it had solid sales figures and had a devoted fan base. I drowned my sorrows in countless glasses of chocolate milk.

Another comic book title I enjoyed was *Joker*. It was unusual for super-villains to have their own series: the only other one I was aware of was *Tomb of Dracula: TOD*, which featured the atmospheric art of Gene "The Dean" Colan and the writing of Marv Wolfman, who also scripted *Nova*. While *TOD* had a 70-issue run, *Joker* was cancelled after 9 issues. By the time I started reading the Joker's comic, it had been cancelled for over a year. Still, that it existed was a great joy, and it was Grandmother Mary who gave me a copy of the fifth issue of *Joker*. The plot of the issue finds an actor who is playing Sherlock Holmes in a play. The actor gets hit in the head. When he comes to, the actor believes that he is actually Sherlock Holmes. The Joker tries to pull off a crime, but is foiled by the actor.

"Elementary," Grandmother Mary said as we finished reading it together. "I can't see his moustache here," she said. Then she started to cackle. It was a higher pitched, yet raspier version of my father's laugh. Caesar Romero said it well: "A joke a day keeps the gloom away."

* * *

When Grandmother Mary died, years passed before I purchased another comic book. I thought of her every time I saw one, which made my heart hurt. Some days you just can't get rid of a bomb.

This changed when I lived in Northeast Ohio. My partner Beth and I found a comic shop that had some wonderful books, including *Nova's* origin issue, and the fifth issue of *Joker*. Not only were these comics in great condition, they only cost a dollar a piece. This shop also had hundreds of back issues in the middle of the store, which was known as "the quarter bin," as every comic in it cost 25 cents. I felt my eyes bulge out of my sockets.

I felt like the archaeologist Howard Carter after he saw King Tutankhamen's tomb for the first time. I found some Batman comics from the 1960's. I also found some back issues of *The Amazing Spider-Man*, *Green Lantern*, and *Tomb of Dracula*. Some of these comics had scuffed covers and corners, but more than a few of them looked as if they had never been read.

When I came up for air, I had about 100 comics or so, all of which formed the nucleus of my comic book collection's rebirth. Some of the books were ones that I had owned before, having bought them myself or having received them as gifts from Grandmother Mary.

As much as I enjoy their artwork and stories, what I have come to realize is that these particular comics are splendid permission slips that allow me to focus on some of the best parts of my childhood. I feel as if I reconnect with Grandmother Mary when I read them; her ear-to-ear smile warming the drafty room as we read together on her navy blue and hot pink floral-patterned couch, peanut butter stuck to the roof of my mouth.

Dual Role

If there's a Heaven, I hope that it's full of popcorn and cinema. One of the reasons why I enjoy watching movies is because I often do so in the company of others. Whether I'm at home or at a theatre, there is something about the shared experience of screening a movie at the same time with family, friends, and strangers alike that appeals to me. One of the more memorable cases in point took place in the Summer of 1980, when I saw *The Final Countdown: Countdown* with my parents.

I liked the idea of *Countdown* more than the finished product. The movie revolves around the intrepid crew of U.S.S. Nimitz, a United States Navy aircraft carrier. The Nimitz goes through a time vortex, which transports them to December 6, 1941, the day before the Pearl Harbor invasion. This presents a moral conundrum: should the Nimitz, armed with state-of-the-art weaponry, circa 1980, ward off the Japanese air assault, or should they refrain, knowing that such an act might change the proverbial course of American history forever? What to do?

My father chain smoked and munched popcorn with gusto throughout *Countdown.* His longest drags and quickest, loudest munches and crunches came when the actors James Farentino and Martin Sheen were on the screen. In *Countdown,* Sheen plays Lasky, an observer employed by Mr. Tideman, whose company made the Nimitz. Tideman orders Lasky to go on board the Nimitz and see how things are operating. Farentino plays Commander Owens, one of the Nimitz's main officers. Then comes the vortex. Pearl Harbor. Fight scenes. Melodrama. Shock and disbelief. And more. Get your popcorn ready.

"Lookit, Mojo," my father said, when Commander Owens first appeared in *Countdown.* "There's James Farentino! He's Italian. And a Brooklyn guy. We gotta root for him."

*   *   *

In retrospect, my father's words about Farentino were more memorable than any of *Countdown's* dialogue. Nevertheless, I watched with interest as Owens got left behind in 1941, while the rest of the Nimitz's crew and passengers made it back to 1980.

When the Nimitz returned to the 80's, I thought of the movie *The Black Hole,* which I had seen the year before with my parents and sister. The Cygnus, the main vessel and galactic haunted house of that film, also provided the setting, the dramatic nerve center where the majority of its action took place. It is to *The Black Hole* what the Nimitz is to *Countdown.* Both films were interesting to look at it, and their concepts were fascinating. Unfortunately, as was the case with *Countdown, The Black Hole's* dialogue was talky and tedious.

Having first seen these movies in my boyhood, I was all about ideas. Time travel was a topic that *Countdown* and *The Black Hole* worked with in ways that intrigued me. I was a child of the 1970's: the decade when 8 of the first 12 human beings walked on the moon; when going to the moon was considered by some to be routine; when Sci-Fi adventure films such as *Star Wars* and *Star Trek* started their runs as blockbuster franchises and captured filmgoers' imaginations. Studios rushed to make Sci-Fi movies, or ones that had Sci-Fi elements, such as *Countdown.* I can't help but wonder if both, *The Black Hole* and *Countdown* would have been more cogent, resonant, and acclaimed if they had tighter scripts; if they invested more craft and rumination in what the actors said as much as they did on their respective technical aspects, the facts that both movies were profitable notwithstanding. Time travel was where the money was, especially given that a new decade, the 1980's, had begun, one that was about to be defined in the U.S.A. by President Ronald Reagan as "Morning in America;" as a decade where young adults across the country became upwardly mobile, including my parents, who had begun to work longer hours and save money for a down payment for a bigger house on a block where each residence looked the same. Keeping up appearances has always been good business for the (good ol') U.S. of A. and its most influential people.

Movies are a visual medium. A film's look is as least as important as how it speaks and sounds, if not more so. That the Nimitz was an actual US Navy ship gave *Countdown* authenticity. Seeing the actors hit their marks on a ship that was battle-ready was convincing. With his olive skin, dark hair and eyes, James Farentino looked like people I grew up with, which added to the film's appeal to me and my parents, especially in the film's big reveal: Mr. Tideman is the elderly self of Commander Owens. Even more than the time travel plot device, this is *Countdown's* main gimmick, which delighted my father beyond measure.

"Two roles! Farentino played *two* roles. Columbus—an Italian discovered America, and another one rescues it. Madone!"

* * *

Decades later, *Countdown* strikes me as a missed opportunity. If the film's production and writing teams wanted to make a roller-coaster, I submit that they should have purchased stock in Six Flags. I'm not a filmmaker, but having been raised on a steady diet of Steven Spielberg films, I know that it's possible for a film to have the stuff of poignancy and serious bank. While Don Taylor was a fine director, I can't help but feel that a close study and embracement of Spielberg's directorial values might have served *Countdown* (and perhaps his legacy) better. It might have been more than a film of its time. The technical wizardry of its special effects continued the new standard of box-office profits that *Star Wars* had started: blockbusters that were frenetic thrill rides. To paraphrase James Earl Jones in *Star Wars,* I find its lack of substance disappointing.

And yet, I had fun watching *Countdown* when I first saw it. It was the first Martin Sheen performance I saw on a movie screen, which made me appreciate his turn in *Apocalypse Now* when I saw it on cable TV a few years later. That Harrison Ford, who I had come to know from his performances from *Star Wars, The Empire Strikes Back, Raiders of the Lost Ark,* and *American Graffiti,* and Marlon Brando, who I saw play Jor-El in *Superman: The Movie* and Vito Corleone in *The Godfather* were also in *Apocalypse Now,* piqued my interest in their work further. I began to understand the phrase "familiar faces" in new ways from Sheen, via Farentino, Ford and Brando.

Other than Farentino's guest appearances in the TV medical drama *ER,* I saw little else of his post-*Countdown* work. When he died in 2012, I learned that his entertainment career spanned five decades. Farentino earned two Golden Globe nominations, one of which he won in 1967, in the Most Promising Newcomer category for his performance in the 1966 comedy *The Pad and How to Use It.* I thought of his dual role of Commander Owens/Mr. Tideman. My memory was sucked into a vortex. I traveled back to 1980; popcorn bits in my father's moustache; a trail of Benson and Hedges smoke, drifting in the buttery, flat-soda scented, multiplex air.

Wine and Shine

Some movies are not meant for children. Especially after your belly is bloated with all-you-can-eat shrimp, salad, and all-you-can drink sangria. This became clear to me when my parents took my sister Nicole and I to see *The Shining* as part of our weekend ritual of going to dinner at Beefsteak Charlie's and seeing a movie. I was 9. Nicole was 13, and our parents were out of their minds.

From the moment I saw the Rocky Mountains in the film's opening scenes, to the aerial shots above a car as it made its way through snowy, narrow roads, I was terrified. The synthesizer chords were sinister and forceful, and I felt sick. What's more, the camera didn't follow the car so much as it lurked above it. When the opening credits appeared, they slid down the screen, like predators overtaking their prey. I didn't know who was in the car, and I wasn't sure that I wanted to.

Now that I was scared to death of Colorado, I had to look away from the screen. I noticed that there were only two other people in the theatre. A man and a woman sat in the front row of the theatre's center section. My family and I were on the left side of the theatre, about ten rows in, and my seat was closest to the aisle. The theatre itself was seedy. Large paper cups, empty popcorn buckets, M&M boxes, straws and kernels were scattered in our row of seats and throughout the main aisle. The exit sign at the front of the theatre flickered. I didn't see an usher for the entire film. The place looked abandoned.

Perhaps it had something to do with *The Shining's* recurring image of blood rushing out of elevators and flooding the Overlook Hotel hallway. For me, seeing it for the first time was especially terrifying. I remember wanting to find higher ground, out of fear that the blood would flow off the screen to overwhelm the theatre, the parking lot, and Sunrise Highway. I felt short of breath. Nicole and I seemed to be on the same wavelength. We held each other's hand until the next scene.

While Nicole and I were trying to remember to breathe, our parents were smiling and taking drags of their smokes. My mother had read Stephen King's novel, the original version of *The Shining*. He had become one of her favorite authors, and she was curious to see how it would work as a movie. Throw in the all-you-can-drink sangria from dinner, which flowed like the blood on the screen, our parents saw no reason why everyone wouldn't enjoy the film.

Seeing the expressions of intrigue and enjoyment on our parents' faces baffled me. In addition to the graphic violence, *The Shining* was also rated R for its use of profanity. This seemed contradictory, as Nicole and I were "forbidden" to swear. Any time our parents heard us doing so resulted in being slapped or punched, which was often followed up by being sent to bed without dinner and being grounded for a week. We couldn't curse, but it was okay to see a human being hacked to death with an ax and watch the victim's blood and guts splatter onto the floor. They had no qualms about watching people French kiss naked female ghosts, swing baseball bats at each other's heads, chop a door down with said ax or the aforementioned torrential floods of elevator blood, but cursing was prohibited. It was bad enough to be as frightened as I was, but this feeling was exacerbated by confusion. I didn't know which was worse: our parents' obliviousness that Nicole and I were frightened, that they were too involved in the film, or too high to notice.

The Shining introduced me to Jack Nicholson as an actor. My father had talked him up at dinner in between rounds of shrimp and salad. To hear my father tell it, Jack was crazy. And funny: funnier than John Belushi, even. He spoke of Jack's Oscar-winning performance in *One Flew Over the Cuckoo's Nest* with the same reverence that he usually reserved whenever Joe DiMaggio or Yogi Berra's names came up in conversation. Jack was also of Italian and Irish descent, so my father held him in high regard, saying that I would "love him."

I found my father's words about Jack's craziness to be true. In fact, it seemed as if his character, who was also named Jack, was insane from the jump. While I laughed during *The Shining's* iconic and perhaps most quoted scene, where he chops down a bathroom door with an ax and sneers, "Here's Johnny," I was uncomfortable in doing so. It has taken me years to fully appreciate the intensity and talent Jack brought to *The Shining.* Of all of his films, his performances in *Five Easy Pieces* and *One Flew Over the Cuckoo's Nest* are my favorites. Crazy and rebellious is his niche, and it pays well, even in the winter of his career, when he added curmudgeonly to his acting range.

The creepiness and technical virtuosity of *The Shining* made it challenging for me to get into the characters themselves. I remember being somewhat excited at the sight of Tony Burton, who I knew from *Rocky* and *Rocky II,* having played Duke Evers, Apollo Creed's trainer. Still, he only had a handful of lines and scenes. My main memories of Shelly Duvall's portrayal of Wendy Torrance are of her screaming and her eyes, which bulged throughout most of the film. She sounded and looked the way I felt as I was watching it.

Nevertheless, I felt the most empathy for Mr. Hallorann, the hotel's chef, played by the inimitable Scatman Crothers. Like Danny, who was played by Danny Lloyd, Mr. Hallorann also had telepathic abilities, like his grandmother before him, which she called "shining." The scenes where Mr. Hallorann and Danny talk over a bowl of ice cream were a welcome relief from the rest of the gore and psychological terror that Stanley Kubrick inflicted on the audience. The moments when Jack drank bourbon and talked murder with ghosts; when Danny pedaled his Big Wheel bike in The Overlook's long hallways, looked into room 237, and chanted and wrote "redrum" on a bathroom door were all rife with suspense, and raised the film's already stratospheric levels of fear. Although I was glad that Danny and Wendy got away, I hated to see that Jack hacked Mr. Hallorann to death with an ax. All work and no play might have made Jack a dull boy, but seeing Mr. Halloran's corpse, sprawled out on a rug in the Overlook lobby, punctuated a thoroughly disturbing and disconcerting night of dinner and a movie.

When the film ended, I felt like I got parole. My parents asked me what I thought of the film, and all I could say was, "Here's Johnny."

My father laughed. My mother inquired further. Nicole said what I was thinking and would have nightmares about for the next year: "Blood pouring out of elevators. What the hell?"

My mother told us not to worry. *The Shining* we saw was different from the one she read, which she explained was standard practice when books were adapted into films. She encouraged us to discover this for ourselves by reading it. She also spoke of Stanley Kubrick's other films, some of which were worth watching, most notably *2001: A Space Odyssey,* saying that it "helped make *Star Wars, Close Encounters of the Third Kind,* and *E. T.: The Extra-Terrestrial* possible."

* * *

Years would pass before I read *The Shining*. I found Stephen King's novel to be more of a psychological thriller, whereas Stanley Kubrick's film is unsettling. I still have nightmares of drowning in an elevator flooded with blood, but I have come to appreciate the film as a talented artist's take on another and equally talented artist's work.

I also realize that my first viewing of *The Shining* marked a watershed in my family's history. Perhaps more than any other family outing, my parents' decision to take Nicole and I to see the film is indicative of how they tried to be good to us. They thought that the experience would be fun, that it would become "an unforgettable memory" as my mother told me.

Memorable, yes. Fun? *Non cosi tanto:* not so much. In thinking about that night, all I am sure of is that reality and perception merged, and it scared the hell out of me. Although Stephen King wrote the character of Jack Torrance as an alcoholic who gave into his demons, his insanity never developed in Stanley Kubrick's adaptation. It was a matter of fact; it was always present, like the Rockies, and the Native American burial ground that the Overlook Hotel is built on.

Movies like *The Shining* are emotional touchstones; they are products of moments and places that show me where I was at certain points in my life. Watching it takes me back to the seediest movie theatre I have ever been to. It reminds me of a time where I had more feelings than words, which makes me grateful for all of who have taught me ways of expressing myself and inspire me to continue learning how I might do so. It is for this reason that I can say "Here's Johnny" to Nicole and share a good laugh.

Watching *The Shining* also takes me back to Beefsteak Charlie's. Eating my weight in shrimp and salad puts my parents' enjoyment of endless pitchers of sangria in perspective. Recalling their intoxication that night still gives me pause, but it also makes me see them as human beings; as young adults having fun, grateful for the opportunity to live in the moment; not preoccupied with confrontations, finances, or report cards. They anticipated having a good time, in large part because of familiarity: my father with Jack Nicholson's films, my mother with Stephen King's and Stanley Kubrick's respective bodies of work, which they wanted to share with us. For better or worse, Nicole and I have inherited some of their knowledge, along with their physical characteristics, tendencies, and abilities, and we carry on in our own way, like Jack, Stephen, and Stanley: the prospect of driving in the Rockies in winter inducing nausea; the sight of a hotel elevator making hairs on the back of my neck stand on end.

Don't Change

My sister Nicole once told me that I was her first friend. This made me feel ten feet tall. Not only was she popular, her wardrobe was compiled entirely of chic outfits, and more than a few of her friends were pretty, amiable, funny, and well-versed in contemporary music. Every time one of them came over, our parents' living room became a faux leather classroom, where each song and album that played on our father's stereo system was a sonorous lesson in my musical education.

Such was especially the case during the first and only weekend our parents spent in Atlantic City, New Jersey together as husband and wife. They made Nicole the "House Supervisor," which meant that she was responsible for watching my then-infant brother John and me and for being sure that our digs were "neat and cleanly upon our arrival home," as our mother put it.

While Nicole resolved not to be derelict in her duty, her first act as House Supervisor was to invite "a few guests" over as soon as our parents hit the road.

The first invited guest arrived about an hour after our parents left. Her name was Kris. She was the newest, nicest, and best-looking member of Nicole's ever-growing crew. She had shoulder-length blond hair, emerald-green eyes, a devilish grin, and eclectic tastes in music. Kris had a particular fondness for the Australian rock band INXS, whose album *Shabooh Shoobah* had just been released.

Nicole was on the phone, so Kris put *Shabooh Shoobah* on my father's stereo turntable. I sat on the sofa and pretended to look at the album cover while she danced the gold paint off of the ceramic bull on top of the TV set. By the end of the album, I had a new appreciation for the use of a synthesizer solo at the start of a song, the potent, come-hither lead vocals of Michael Hutchence, the album's final song "Don't Change," and purple striped shorts.

Then Paula, Nicole's doe-eyed second invited guest, came over later that night. At Paula's suggestion, Nicole made popcorn on the stovetop, using our mother's favorite stock pot, which was used primarily for making pasta and Sunday sauce. I could taste Orville Redenbacher's Original Gourmet Popcorn, fluffy with butter on my tongue.

Kris sang along with Michael Hutchence. Paula laughed, and the smoke alarm joined in with its red, high-pitched voice.

The bitter smell of burnt popcorn filled the hallway. My concerns chirped in the smoke alarm as I joined Nicole, Kris, and Paula in the kitchen.

Nicole removed the pot's lid, and flames promptly shot up to the ceiling and licked the walls of the kitchen.

"Fire," Kris yelled. She went to the freezer and grabbed some ice cubes.

"Stand back, everyone," she said.

Paula's eyes widened. "No wait! Don't"—

Kris threw ice cubes in the pot. More flames rose up to the ceiling and the walls. I felt my face and was amazed that my eyebrows hadn't been incinerated.

Nicole put the lid back on the pot. Then she grabbed the pot and put it in the sink, and ran some cold water on it. Paula took the battery out of the alarm.

Kris opened the kitchen window. The pot smoldered, and braids of smoke slithered through the screen.

"Holy crap," Paula said as she looked at my mother's pasta pot. "It's like looking at the inside of a demented chimney."

Nicole rubbed her chin. "I'm going to need a big sponge," she said.

"Don't worry," Kris said. "We'll help you clean up."

"Go check on John," Nicole said to me. "Now. And stay with him."

I went into John's room and mine. He rubbed his eyes, so I took him out of his crib and changed his diaper before we both fell asleep.

The ringing of the house phone woke me up. Midnight arrived

like the Grim Reaper. I went back into the kitchen, or what was left of it. I hoped that my mother wasn't calling to check in.

Kris picked it up. Apparently, she and Paula had invited their boyfriends over.

"Don't worry. We're having a party. Nicole's P's are in Atlantic City. We already burned the kitchen down."

*　*　*

Nicole and her guests scrubbed through the night. I went into the kitchen to see if I could help.

Paula looked at the watch on her left wrist. "Is it really 8 O'clock? I'm done. Overdone, like this damned popcorn. Tell me how everything turns out."

Kris slammed down her sponge. "We need to stay and help our friend!"

Paula furrowed her eyebrows. "What do you think I've been doing all night and morning? Splitting atoms at Los Alamos? Like I said, tell me how it turns out. Call me later."

Nicole, who was standing on one of the kitchen countertops, hopped down. She patted my shoulder.

"Come. I have a job for you," she said. "Kris, hand Jojo the bag."

The Demented Chimney was in a Hefty plastic bag. It smelled like lemons and gasoline. I started to cough.

"Take it to the sump," Nicole said.

"The Sump" referred to Memorial Sump, the watery pit that was located at the bottom of the hill behind Memorial Junior High School's baseball field. It was two blocks away from our house and was our neighborhood's Studio 54. All of the local cool kids and badasses gathered there on summer nights to get stoned, fight, and have sex in the woods behind the sump. Adults used the sump itself as a landfill for all kinds of objects, including lampshades, shotgun barrels, and prosthetic legs. My task was clear: the Demented Chimney was to "go the way of the Andrea Doria," after the SS Andrea Doria disaster of 1956, when 52 people died en route to New York City.

"Be sure it sinks," Nicole said. "Don't just throw it in there. Got it?"

As Michael Hutchence sang, the message was received loud and clear. I rode my bicycle to Memorial Sump, which was filled to the rim with rainwater. The fence was almost two feet taller than me. Some of the chain link went over the metal railing, including some tips, which were like wild, rusted metallic hairs. I tried to figure out how I might haul the bag over it. I didn't want to miss the water, so I had to be sure that I could make a good throw.

There was one other problem. While the popcorn kernels stuck to the bottom of the Demented Chimney had increased its weight, it wasn't heavy enough to sink to the bottom of the sump. Given all of the trash and broken objects strewn about, there had to be something I could use to help it sink.

The answers presented themselves in the forms of two bricks and a milk crate. The crate reeked of cat piss. The smell was dreadful, but the prospect of Nicole's and my mother's combined wrath resolved me to use it as a makeshift footstool and press on.

I put the bricks inside the Demented Chimney and put it in the bag. After I double knotted the bag, I stepped on the crate of cat piss and hurled it over the fence.

Kerplunk! Mission accomplished. I saw Michael Hutchence, strutting up and down my mind's stage as I hopped on my bicycle. I saw no evil in all directions.

I took a deep breath, and took a moment to calm down before I went home. For some reason, I thought about Memorial Junior High's parking lot, where my father had taught me how to ride my bicycle. I had gone from falling off to using it to get rid of incriminating evidence of a killed stock pot.

Even though my father was in Atlantic City, I could hear him yelling, "Get your ass up! Pedal!" I had fallen off more times than I could count, and most of my friends rode their Mongoose, Red Line, and Diamond Back BMX bicycles more adroitly than I could walk. As is the case with most things, I am a late bloomer. I am also a slow learner, but once I get the hang of something, if it ever happens—it usually stays with me. Having grown up in a place where everything seemed to move at a breakneck pace, it was a challenge to keep up with my friends and their families. Learning how to ride a bicycle, and ride it well, was one of my first lessons in individuality; that people learn in different ways and rates, and it's okay.

I looked at my watch. An hour had passed since I left home. "Nicole is probably fuming," I thought. Get your ass up. Pedal.

When I returned to the house, the kitchen walls and ceiling were cleaner. A couple of faint streaks of soot aside, the room was neat and cleanly. Nicole had bags under her eyes.

John kicked happily in his high chair as Kris fed him. At 2 years old, my kid brother was a charmer. He still is. Don't change a thing.

I assured Nicole that the Demented Chimney was put to rest. She informed me that our parents had called to inform us that they were on their way home, as our father had "won big at the slot machines."

"I'll vacuum," Nicole said. "You help Kris take care of John."

*　*　*

Kris was gone by the time my parents came home. I was playing with John when I heard my mother's voice. Nicole was making small talk with her in the kitchen.

"Boy oh boy," Nicole said. "How about tonight's sky, huh? I mean, is that a lavender sky or what?"

I carried John into the kitchen. My parents planted kisses on his forehead and nose. The window was still open, and I saw two green purses from "The Playboy Club" on the table. They were filled with quarters, which were exhibits A and B of just how great of a time my parents seemed to have in Atlantic City, which my father called "A.C."

"Hey! Joefish! Look at all these quarters," my father said. "I just love A.C."

Our mother studied the walls. "It looks like you guys have been busy, making the house look as neat and cleanly as it does."

John drooled on my chest. "Thanks, Ma," Nicole said. "We tried. Right, Jojo?"

"And how," I said.

Then my mother scrutinized the ceiling. "The ceiling looks different, doesn't it, Joe?" She said to our father. "Boy, you guys went all out, didn't you?"

"Yeah," my father said. "It almost looks as good as the one in our A.C. hotel room. Ha!"

My mother rolled her eyes. Then she looked at Nicole and yawned.

"Well, I need a shower, and we need dinner. Can you order pizza, Nicole? Two Sicilian pies from Francesco's?"

"Great idea, Marie," my father said. This calls for a smoke!"

My father lit a Camel cigarette. John's eyes watered. Our mother sighed. "Give me your brother," she said.

John flashed a toothless smile as our mother dried his eyes and mouth.

"You go on and get comfortable, Ma. I'll take care of everything, " Nicole said.

Nicole smiled, and then dialed Francesco's number. Our parents vanished down the hallway; our mother with John in her arms, my father's Camel leaving a trail of smoke behind them.

People of Faith

I believe that Annie Lennox sang it well: everybody's looking for something. When I was in my tweens, it seemed as if my sister Nicole's greatest wish was that she could host a party at our family's home. She spent countless hours asking and pleading with our parents to have one, only to be refuted each time.

When I was 12, Nicole formulated a new way of getting permission to have her party. This time, she decided to include a starting and end time for the party: from 7:00 pm—10:00 pm, so that it wasn't too early or late in the day or night. She would also ask if our parents wouldn't mind being chaperones, so that they could keep an eye on things. Our grandparents, Joe and Mary: our father's parents, who lived in the downstairs area of our house, could also help out. Perhaps, Nicole surmised, if Uncle Steve, my father's best friend, came to the party, he could be another chaperone to help monitor things, which might assure them, and especially our mother, that everything would proceed without incident. The more trusted adults that were present at the party, the merrier.

It worked. Our parents gave Nicole the green light, on the condition that they would oversee all aspects of it. "No parents, no party," was how our mother put it. "Also, whatever I say goes. No questions asked."

Nicole agreed, and didn't stop smiling for weeks. It was the happiest I had seen her in the entirety of our years together in our family's Teed Street digs. Grandfather Joe offered usage of his records, tapes, and Hi-Fi system, and Grandmother Mary volunteered to help Nicole prepare food and help her in any other way that she needed or wanted. I also volunteered my services. I would keep an eye on John, our brother, who was a toddler at the time.

Not only did Nicole accept, she also told me that I could invite one of my friends to her bash. I couldn't say "thank you" enough.

"Totally," she said. "Just don't call it a 'bash.' Deal?"

I was excited on Nicole's behalf. I was also pumped because I would get to hang out with Amy, Uncle Steve's daughter, who Nicole also planned on inviting, as well as the rest of her friends, some of whom I got to know over the years, and who always treated me with kindness, respect, and a genuine interest in how I was doing.

Nicole had also recently joined a church youth group, where she had made some new friends, including Kris, who I had a crush on. My parents were pleased that Nicole was hanging out with "people of faith," particularly my mother, whose relationship with Nicole was contentious, at best. The youth group factor also appealed to my father's religious sensibilities, for as light-hearted as he was, he took his faith seriously, often referring to Catholicism as being "The real religion." I had no idea what that meant. I still don't.

* * *

Not-bash time. Grandmaster Melle Mel's "White Lines" (Don't Do It) blasted from Grandfather Joe's stereo speakers, both of which were situated in his and Grandmother Mary's kitchen window. Curt Rivers, my sister's best male friend, guffawed in between sips of punch. The bug lamp spat out mosquitoes and flies at will. Nicole was smiling from ear to ear as she walked through the crowd of people crammed into our backyard. My mother was behind the white metallic patio door, a stern expression on her face, her arms akimbo.

My friend Matty-Ass made his way toward Donna, one of Nicole's besties. I adjusted the bill of my Lilac-purple pageboy hat. Liz, our cross-street neighbor, sat on top of the patio table.

I kicked it with my sister's friend Herbie, who I met for the first time. Herbie had a moustache like Prince and a physique like Willie Randolph, the New York Yankees' All-Star second baseman. He was one of Nicole's youth group friends, and was a DJ in Dancetaria, a club in New York City's Upper West Side. I remember him looking through my stack of 45 records and albums, and pulling out The Police's "Every Little Thing She Does is Magic."

"Nice choice. Sting's the man, little man," he said. "If you like that song, listen to this." The Police's then-current hit song "Every Breath You Take" thumped from the stereo.

"You hear that bassline? People will use this forever. Believe it."

Then Paul, Nicole's boyfriend, showed up. He was also in Nicole's youth group, and a star pitcher for Nicole's varsity high school baseball team. They had been going out for about six months, and seemed to be into each other. I remember that Nicole had started a scrapbook compiled of news clippings and box scores of his baseball games.

I didn't know Paul well, but something about him gave me pause. I remember that his that his shoelaces were often untied. Matty-Ass also wasn't sold on Paul, noting that "his breath was sour, and he talked 200 miles an hour. Faster than his fastball."

Still, Paul and I exchanged quick waves of hello before Nicole gave him a big hug. My mother glared. Eurythmics' "Sweet Dreams (Are Made of This)" pulsed through the backyard. Then Uncle Steve made his entrance. He had a can of Miller Lite beer in one hand and a smoke in the other. We made eye contact, and he made a "shh" gesture with his smoke hand.

He pulled out a couple of facial tissues, looked around, and then stuffed both of them in one of his nostrils. Then he walked up to Donna and tapped her on the shoulder.

"Guess who I am?"

Sue furrowed her eyebrows.

"Any idea, buddy?" he asked Matty-Ass.

"Biggs Darklighter with a bad cold?"

Uncle Steve laughed in spite of himself. Then he made a series of peculiar roaring noises. He sounded like a Velociraptor being pressed through a meat grinder. He kept it up for about a minute, though it felt longer. The reactions ranged from nervous laughter to expressions of disgust and bewilderment.

"I'm the Elephant Man," Uncle Steve said. "Get it?"

Donna smirked and rolled her eyes. Matty-Ass burst out laughing, as did most of the men who heard the punchline, including Grandfather Joe, who spat out his drink. Kris smiled and crossed herself.

"Dad," Amy yelled. "Again with that stupid joke? What the vanilla fuck?"

Uncle Steve smirked. "Be careful, Honey. People are gonna get the wrong idea about you if you talk dirty like that."

"Where's the problem?" Grandfather Joe said.

"Keep your pants on, King Farouk," Grandmother Mary said.

My mother took a deep sigh and stomped back into the house. She slammed the white metal door behind her. It became unhinged.

"Right on," Herbie said. "Now it's a party!"

* * *

Matty-Ass bounced. I finally had the chance to talk to Kris. We were surprised by the abrupt stop to Michael Jackson's song Beat It.

My mother was apparently uninterested in who was wrong or right. She made her way to the middle of the patio, and clapped her hands.

"Ok, kiddies," she called out. "It's time to go home. Time to leave kiddies. That's it." Nicole took a deep breath. "What are you saying? It's not 9 O'clock yet."

It was just after 8 O'clock, as Kris showed me on her hot pink watch. My mother clapped her hands and repeated herself, as if Nicole hadn't said anything.

"Why are you doing this, Ma?" Nicole asked.

My mother cleared her throat. "I told you, no questions asked."

Nicole was stupefied. Amy took her hand, and they left the backyard together.

"Is it okay if I stay, Marie?" Uncle Steve asked.

Then he pulled out a Snickers candy bar from one of his pockets and held it out for my mother's consideration.

"You want a Snickers? They really satisfy—like me!"

My mother glared at Uncle Steve. My father laughed, which did not go unnoticed.

"Jesus Fucking Christ, Joe," my mother said. "Help me get the kiddies out of here."

"Ok, Marie," my father said. " Just one thing. I love you. Even more than candy."

My mother sighed and began asking some of Nicole's guests to "vacate the premises." My father and Uncle Steve exchanged gestures of shrugged shoulders. Mosquitoes drifted towards the bug lamp.

Then my mother glared at me. "Go to your room and check on your brother. Now!"

I hauled ass. Not only was John, asleep, he was snoring so loudly, his crib was rattling. I felt a burst of laughter forming in my throat, which made me cover my mouth and walk out of our room quietly.

I somehow made my way into the living room without making too much noise. I allowed myself a chuckle and looked out the front window. The driveway was packed with my sister's guests. Uncle Steve, Paul, and my father led everyone to the shoreline of our driveway. I saw Herbie give the thumbs up sign to Curt and Paul before they vanished into the sea of teenagers and whips in the street.

The streetlight in front of our house turned on. My mother walked up the front stoop. I scurried back into mine and John's room and hopped into bed. I put my hat on my bedside table, closed my eyes, and prayed silently.

Our father, who art in heaven, please don't let my mother kill my sister or me; please don't let her kill us. Let Nicole, Amy, Kris, Donna, Liz, Curt, Herbie and the rest of her friends have a good time someplace else tonight. Perhaps at Dancetaria. Amen.

I opened my eyes and stared at the ceiling, as if it would explain why my mother ended the party early. She and Nicole seemed to have gotten on well until my mother's sudden order of dispersion. I wanted to ask her what the problem was, but the furious look in her eyes and the tone of lit dynamite in her voice silenced me.

My father and Uncle Steve interrupted my thoughts. Their voices carried as they made themselves comfortable in the living room. My mother stomped behind them: it ended once she went into the bathroom and locked herself in. I stared at the ceiling's plastered calligraphy, hopeful that it would help me find some answers, such as how to drown out the slamming of doors in the bathroom; the red, white, and green screams of cars peeling out of the driveway and speeding down Teed Street; my father's and Uncle Steve's cackles and guffaws like background vocals to John's loud, frontman snoring.

Catch You Later

My father was bored. The novelty of watching movies without commercials had worn off for him faster than he could say HBO. After a few months of enjoying the opportunity to watch some of his favorite movies, such as *West Side Story* on cable television, he didn't always get to see them, on account of being at work when they were aired. More often than not, he saw parts of movies, instead of their entirety, which frustrated him, which was exacerbated by the fact that he was paying for the service.

This created a desire for him to have greater agency in what we watched and when he could watch it. He and my mother were saving money to move into a bigger house, which they determined was necessary after my brother John was born. This meant that we no longer went out to dinner and a movie together. Our kitchen and living room became our de facto restaurant and movie theatre. This also meant that he had to pick up more bus driving shifts for the Metropolitan Transit Authority. Watching movies after work had become his go-to activity for unwinding after long days of driving strangers and picking them up throughout New York City, which necessitated a considerable amount of time to be spent in commuting to and from our home, which he wasn't able to spend nearly as much time at as he wanted to. If he had to work as much as he and my mother felt that he did, he was also going to find a way to enjoy himself from time to time, to control as much as he could, morning, city, rush hour traffic, and HBO programming schedules be damned.

A remedy presented itself in the proliferation of the Video Cassette Recorder, the VCR, which had become a popular American household item in the early 1980's. The more my father talked about it, the more excited he was to have one; to record movies on Video Home System, VHS tapes. The convenience of having a VCR that recorded a particular movie or show he wanted to see when he wasn't able to watch it made him giddy. He expressed this to me by likening VHS tapes to the cassettes I used to make "mix-mash tapes" of my favorite music.

"Let me put it this way, Joefish," he said. "You can be like that Phil Collins guy and turn it on again. And again."

My father's enthusiasm for the prospect of getting a VCR was infectious. This period of my life had moments of hope: moments where it seemed as if everyone in my nuclear family might enjoy each other's company for more than a day or part of a night.

For me, the most memorable example of this way this was when my sister, mother, and I decided to get my father a VCR for a Father's Day gift. We resolved to find a VCR that we thought he'd like: ideally one with a remote control, and one that we could all afford if we split its cost three ways. I was excited to collaborate.

Operation VCR went off without a hitch. We shopped around: we looked in every department store and electronics shop in town over the course of a month or so. My mother, who deposited my paper route money in a bank account that I wasn't allowed to access, decreed that some of my paychecks would go towards the VCR. "When your Father's happy, everyone else will be, too," she said. "It'll be a worthy sacrifice."

The search yielded a Sharp VCR, which had a green button for play, a red button for stop, and of course, a remote control. We were pleased with the button color schemes, thinking it to be a sort of inside joke, seeing as how all the VCR needed was a yellow button for slowing things down. My mother laughed as she considered whether or not my father would get the joke. "Stop and go. That describes your father perfectly," she said.

Watching my father's eyes widen as he saw the Sharp box beneath the wrapping paper was truly a sight to behold. Sweat streamed down his red face and neck as he tore off the wrapping paper off the box.

"How about this, Joefish?" He said. "Looking Sharp, Marie!"

He took particular delight in the VCR's remote control: the remote, as he called it. He chuckled every time he pressed the rewind and pause buttons. He couldn't get enough of seeing a film's scene and stopping it to take a closer look at it. Sometimes he hit the pause button so he could light a new smoke.

And yet, he could not sustain his joy. Within a week, he started complaining about the remote. At issue: the remote had to be attached to the VCR to function. He took it back to the store exchanged it for a different VCR, one whose remote was wireless, which was more expensive, and had gray buttons. We had no idea that he did this until he told my mother, me, and siblings.

"Isn't this great, Marie? I mean, look at this beautiful machine, guys!"

My mother was not impressed. "The kids and I worked hard to find a VCR for you," she said.

"I know. But it's a Father's Day present, right?"

My mother sighed. "What's your point, Joe?"

"That means that I should get what I want. I'm the father of this house. My day, my way."

"That's bullshit," I said.

"Joseph!" my mother said.

My father raised his left eyebrow. Then my mother put her hand on my shoulder.

"I think Joefish means that he feels bad that we didn't get you what you wanted. I do, too."

My father smirked. "Thank God for my wife, Joefish."

I furrowed my brow. "Your wife?'

"Yeah, Joefish," my father said. "My wife."

I shook my head. "Why do you do that?"

"Say what now?"

"Why do you call Mom 'Your wife?"

"Because that's what she is. You remember that."

I furrowed my brow. "Believe me, I know that you and Mom are married. That's why I exist."

"That won't be the case for much longer if you keep talking," my father said.

"My mother, your wife. My money or my life," I said.

"Don't get smart."

"Whatever."

"Whatever?" My father said. He clenched his hands into fists and raised them in the air, as if he was the Incredible Hulk, getting ready to smash. "I'll give you whatever!"

"Joe," my mother said, "Why don't we talk more about this in the bedroom?"

"Aww right! Have fun, Dad," I said.

"Madone! You got a mouth on you! What part of your mother, my wife don't you understand?"

"I'm sorry, Dad. We'll always have Paris."

My father looked at me as if I had turned into a pile of sawdust before his blood-shot eyes. My mother kissed his scratched knuckles and took his hand. "I tell you, Marie, that kid's seen too many movies."

*   *   *

Of all the movies my father recorded, the one that stands out the most is *Blue Thunder,* which was the first one he recorded on a VHS tape. *Blue Thunder* is an action-drama starring Roy Scheider as Frank Murphy, a former Vietnam War helicopter pilot who works for the Los Angeles Police Department. Frank is the pilot of Blue Thunder, a state of the art helicopter designed for combat and security. The movie also featured Malcolm McDowell as Colonel F.E. Cochrane, Murphy's adversary, who I had recently seen in Stanley Kubrick's adaptation of *A Clockwork Orange.*

My father had seen *Blue Thunder* prior to making his tape of it. He gave it two thumbs up, the film critics Gene Siskel and Roger Ebert proud. He was excited to record it as they were to review the films of their day.

"Grab a hold of something, Joefish," he said. "If you liked Malcolm or Roy in *Clockwork* or *Jaws,* wait until you see 'em in SP mode."

SP is an acronym for "Standard Play," a two-hour recording capacity for a VHS tape. SP was also the highest quality a program could be recorded in, and at a running time of one hour and 49 minutes, *Blue Thunder* had a perfect fit for the setting. The quality of my father's VHS tape of it was impeccable. It was also a reflection of the paradigm shift that had occurred between us.

I had mixed feelings about this. As much as I missed my relationship with my father for what it used to be, light-hearted, fun, and trusting, I was concerned about what it was turning into. Seeing him with his VHS tapes gave me hope that maybe we could reclaim a semblance of the halcyon days of our relationship when I was a child; less contrary; when he was better rested; less burdened and overwhelmed by increased work commitments; before I was compelled to say whatever I felt or thought without any filtration.

I watched *Blue Thunder* with John and my parents. This made my viewing of the film conspicuous in itself. That it occurred in the afternoon instead of at night, with the insistent whirr of the air conditioner; the leaking of hazy sunlight through cracks of our tobacco-stained living room curtains amplified the viewing's peculiarity.

As much as I enjoy Roy Scheider's and Malcolm McDowell's respective bodies of work; as pimped out with guns and other war machinery as *Blue Thunder's* helicopter was, I found the film to be otherwise forgettable, save for one line of dialogue, which was spoken by both, Roy and Malcolm: "Catch you later."

Roy's rendition of the line stands out to me, on account of when it occurs in the film and my father's reaction to it. In the final act of *Blue Thunder,* Roy's and Malcom's characters Murphy and Cochrane have a helicopter chase sequence, which culminates in the explosion of the latter's helicopter.

"Ha! I can't wait to watch this again! Catch you later!"

My father's cackle fell in fiery debris to the Los Angeles ground. Braids of Benson and Henson smoke slithered around the ceramic red bull with gold horns on top of our TV.

John screamed and cried. My mother took him out of his playpen and left the living room. I didn't see either of them until we ate dinner.

My father smiled from ear to ear as he stabbed into his Swanson Hungry-Man Salisbury steak. A meal of Rat Turd Parmigiana could have maintained his spirits that night.

"What a day," my father said. "It's good to be modern. And full."

Then he raised his glass of 7-Up and Riunite Lambrusco: his spritzer. "Here's to our first homemade movie. To Blue Thunder. And more spritzer. Ha!"

My father belched. John giggled. My mother rolled her eyes.

"Just think," my father said. "You can watch *Blue Thunder* anytime you want. We don't need no stinkin' video shops. It's all ours, for all hours."

In retrospect, the combination of John's birth, my parents working more hours, and their desire to be upwardly mobile hastened our breakup as a family. Their decision to subscribe to cable television started a procession of films that I saw with one of my siblings, parents, or by myself. Coupled with the purchase of a VCR and the way my father used it, movie watching had steadily devolved from a shared experience to an act of isolation. Catch you later.

I haven't seen *Blue Thunder* in decades. When I talk with my father, I sometimes feel like asking him if he's watched it recently; if he has streamed it; if he enjoys the film just as much now as he did when he first taped it; if he enjoys it even more now that he's retired; now that he can watch it or any other movie in its entirety whenever his heart desires. I also feel like asking him if he misses going to dinner and a movie with our nuclear family.

Then I think better of it. I keep these thoughts to myself. I imagine him alone in his living room, sitting in his indigo velour bathrobe, watching TV, pressing the buttons on his remote control like a crazed accountant, smiling like a satisfied lion when he sees and hears Rita Moreno in *West Side Story*, singing about life in America on his state-of-the-art, New York City-sized flat screen.

Bafangool Day

There are holidays that invent themselves. One example is September 17th, which is the birthday of John Franco, the former Houston Astros, Cincinnati Reds, and New York Mets All-Star Closer. Although I was never a Francophile, I have celebrated his birthday every year since 1985, when I met him at Shea Stadium: Big Shea. I do so by eating a big pretzel, shotgunning a bottle of Miller Lite, and toasting him with three words: "Bafongool, John Franco," which roughly translates into, "Up your ass, John Franco." Since that time, September 17th has come to be known as "Bafongool Day" in my house.

My interaction with Franco has led me to believe that T.S. Eliot had a point when he wrote, "April is the cruelest month." I was at Big Shea, watching the Mets play the Cincinnati Reds, which is to say that I was there to see the legendary Reds' player-manager Pete Rose inch closer to surpassing Ty Cobb as Major League Baseball's all-time hits leader. I was chomping at the bit to see Rose do it, as he had long been one of my favorite ballplayers, and I wanted to witness a watershed moment in the game's history.

A die-hard New York Yankees fan, my father surprised me with a pair of tickets a few days before the game, which had been sold out for weeks. I was amped, going so far as to buy a Reds cap and a baseball for Rose to sign. Our seats were in the right field upper deck, or "Nosebleed East," as my father called them, where we had a better view of Big Shea's parking lot behind the outfield fence than the playing field. Once my father started chatting up the people sitting beside us, I grabbed my ball and got up to leave. It was go time, as in time to go meet Rose, Major League Baseball's soon-to-be career hits king.

"Don't take any shit off that Commie bastard," my father said. "And get me some peanuts while you're at it. Two bags."

I inched my way down the network of escalators, through the crowd at the concession and souvenir stands, to the gate that accessed the visitor's dugout. There was no usher, so I ran down the field level tunnel.

Then a bony finger tapped my shoulder. "Ticket, please."

The finger belonged to a short, stocky usher, whose name "Al" seemed to shout from his name tag. With his olive-skin and dashing moustache, he reminded me of my Grandfather Joe.

"Your ticket, please," Al said.

I reached for my stub and handed it to him. It was wrapped in a twenty-dollar bill.

"Please may I go down to the dugout?"

"Okay, little man. Be my guest," Al said. "For ten more dollars."

"Ten more?"

"That's right. Unless you want me to call security."

To my pubescent mind, the chance to see Rose play in person occurred with Halley's Comet-like frequency. Plus, I had no interest in dealing with any variety of the PoPo or my father's reaction to such a turn of events, which would not be pleasant. I gave him the ten.

"Okay, little man," Al said, pressing buttons on his wristwatch. "You got 10 minutes. My colleagues and I will come and get you if you don't leave on your own. Capisce?"

He led me to the front row seats adjacent to the visitor's dugout. I joined a group of 50 or so people. I was at the left end of the row, watching the sea of players, the umpiring crew, newspaper reporters and broadcast journalists. I wondered about how many benjamins Al had scored.

Then Rose emerged from the dugout. He grinned as he walked over to the fence, where a forest of hands holding out baseballs, photographs, yearbooks, and pens awaited him. My heart was beating on the roof of my mouth, but I summoned the courage to speak. This was my chance to put my money where my aorta was.

"Hello, Mr. Rose. I know that you're busy at the moment, but please may I have your autograph? I hope you get closer to breaking Ty Cobb's record today."

"So, ya want my autograph, do ya?" Rose asked.

He fixed his glare on my Reds cap. He seemed to be scrutinizing it, as if it was evidence—exhibit C, so to speak—at a murder trial.

Then he rolled his eyes. My knees knocked. "Get lost."

My heart slid down my throat. I watched in disbelief as Rose sauntered back into the dugout.

Al poked my shoulder blade. "Y'know," he said, "I'll give you five more minutes to hang here if you want." It felt like a stick-up.

I reached for my wallet. "Fuhgedaboudit. On the house," he said. "Lookit. Maybe he changed his mind."

Rose re-emerged and walked to first base. He turned his attention toward the batting cage, where the Reds players were taking pre-game swings. John Cafferty and the Beaver Brown Band's "On the Dark Side" crackled from Big Shea's PA system.

By the time Michael Antunes' rollicking saxophone solo sprayed the infield dirt, I became alerted to presence of the Reds pitchers Jay Tibbs and John Franco. They stood about two feet behind Rose and faced the crowd, which struck me as unusual. Most ballplayers I had seen in person would barely acknowledge the fans before a game, save a quick wave or greeting. Their arms were akimbo, and the looks in their eyes suggested that they meant business, even though people in the crowd were clamoring for their attention. With their red satin warm-up jackets and careful, steady gaits and stillness, Tibbs and Franco reminded me of a big-league baseball version of the Emperor's Royal Guard in *Return of the Jedi*, and their message was implicit: Palpatine Rose was not to be disturbed or harassed.

"Lookit, there's John Franco," Al said. "If Rose won't give you an autograph, maybe John will."

Franco swaggered towards the fence. "Hey, John," Al shouted. "Come stai? How you doin?"

The crowd went insane. Arms reached out like weeds as Franco reached the stands. He might have been on an opposing team, but having been born and raised in Bensonhurst, Brooklyn and a star ballplayer at Lafayette High School and St. John's University, he was a local product who had succeeded in his chosen profession. Franco's success gave fans like Al and other New York baseball fans of Italian lineage sense of hope, that talent and persistence could enable people to rise above their working-class roots and leave their old neighborhoods; their *ghetti* permanently and live la dolce vita, rather than spend the rest of their days relegated to a life of work and responsibility.

Franco smiled and slapped some of the fans' hands. Then it occurred to me that my father just might like having a baseball autographed by Franco. I thought that it would be a way of reciprocating his kindness; of expressing my gratitude for him getting tickets to the game and spending the day at Big Shea with me, especially given his Yankees fandom. I resolved to ask Franco for his John Hancock as soon as he came to where I was standing.

"Hello, Mr. Franco. Welcome back to the city. Please may I have your autograph?"

Franco's smile curled into a smirk. Then he snickered and looked me straight in the eyes.

"Go fuck yourself, kid," he said.

My jaw dropped. I understood that signing autographs was Franco's—or any ballplayer's prerogative, but his sui generis combination of nonchalance and douchebaggery flabbergasted and saddened me.

Then I felt something graze the back of my neck. I looked around: it was an enormous gold crucifix, which dangled like from the chain worn by a fan standing directly behind me.

"You'll never be the man yo momma is, Franco," Gold Crucifix said with blaringly nasal, leather-lunged disdain. "Bafongool!"

Franco's smirk curled into a sneer. He looked straight at Gold Crucifix and I saw his left hand, his pitching hand, curl into a fist. Tibbs motioned to Rose, who in turn motioned to the police officers gathered by the Mets dugout, and then preceded to walk Franco back into the visitor's dugout, slowly and calmly.

"Sorry it didn't work out, little man," Al said. "Enjoy the game."

"Thanks."

"Prego."

My stomach gurgled. I walked up the steps, and then stopped when I got to the exit of the tunnel. I watched Al work. A bald-headed man, a silver-haired woman and a little girl walked up to him. He inspected their tickets. Then he shook the little girl's hand and led the group to their seats, where the adults shared a laugh as they blended into the rest of the crowd seated in the field level section.

I made my way to the nearest concession stand and purchased two bags of peanuts and a big pretzel. People rushed by, arms full of sepia-colored paper trays filled with cheeseburgers and hot dogs; large and small cups of Pepsi-Cola, knishes, and french-fries. I chewed my pretzel and stared at the escalators, teeming with men, women children, and orange foam fingers, the sun glinting off of aviator sunglass lenses, Swatches, and plastic blue Mets batting helmets, the sour smell of Miller Lite melting the cartilage in my nose as tiny hail-stones of salt dissolved on my tongue.

I handed the bags of peanuts to my father and showed him the baseball upon my return. He looked at me with a furrowed brow, but asked no questions. All of my subsequent recollections of the game are a list of curiosities: pain darting through my abdomen; the American flag, flaccid on the pole behind the centerfield wall; the moan of airplanes coming and going above Big Shea; the right field corner of the upper deck bathed in shadow.

Why Not Fred?

Whenever Lady Luck smiles at I me, I try to return it.

For instance, when I was a high school freshman, she gave me the opportunity to meet the New York Islanders' announcer Jiggs McDonald, The New York Mets Third Base Coach Bud Harrelson, and the former New York Yankees reserve outfielder Paul "Motormouth" Blair on the same day. I attended an event where some New York Sports celebrities were giving talks warning against the dangers of drugs as part of then-First Lady Nancy Reagan's "Just Say No" anti-drug abuse campaign. In addition to Jiggs, Bud, and Motormouth, the list of celebrity speakers included the New York Islanders star centers Butch Goring and Pat LaFontaine.

Butch was perhaps most famous to Islander fans for wearing the same helmet he wore since he was 12 years old and for winning the Conn Smythe Trophy as the most valuable player of the 1980 playoffs en route to the winning the first of four consecutive Stanley Cup championships. Butch was his nickname. Robert was his real name.

Pat was the third overall pick in the 1983 NHL Amateur Draft and represented the USA in 1984 Olympics in Sarajevo, Yugoslavia. He had joined the Islanders in time for the 1984 Stanley Cup Final, where the Wayne Gretzky-led Edmonton Oilers defeated them.

Jiggs was the MC of the event, which took place in Half Hollow Hills East High School, or "Hills East," located in Dix Hills, Long Island.

I arrived at Hills East about 45 minutes before the event began. The lobby was teeming with people and I was unsure where I could enter the auditorium. I asked a burly security guard, who pointed towards a line down the hallway, so I went there.

The line had less than 10 people in it. I didn't voice any concerns, because I thought that it was just one of several ways that were being utilized to organize the crowd of people. I recall the echo of a deep, stentorian voice growing in the high school hallway where I stood line and a window at the end of the hall. I kept my eyes posted there, and watched the wind unclench its fist and shove leaves off of trees outside and blanket a parking lot behind the football field. I also took care to check my high tops, laced in an orange and blue checkerboard pattern: colors of New York state, the Mets and Islanders.

My knapsack weighed me down, so I removed it from my shoulder and unzipped it. All of its contents were accounted for: a baseball signed by the former New York Baseball Giants All-Star outfielder Bobby Thomson; a miniature New York Yankees bat; two packs of Big League Chew bubblegum; an ink-stained burgundy Velcro wallet with 25 dollars in cash and three more dollars' worth of quarters.

My yawn clapped in a round of thunder. I dropped my baseball, which rolled towards the front of the line. A tall, steel wool coarse-red-haired boy hands threw it back to me. He then tapped a tall, slender man on the shoulder, who is three spots ahead of me.

"30 minutes, Mr. Blair."

My mind felt like mud, my mouth like glass. Words slid out like water.

"Blair, as in Paul Blair?"

"That's right," the slender man said. "How ya doin?"

I felt the roof of my mouth shatter and heard my voice crack. "I-I'm Joey, Mr. Blair. It's an honor to meet you. You were the man in centerfield."

Mr. Blair smiled. I had also noticed that there were only four people in line: me, a man with gray in his temples is in front of him, and another man with a receding hairline standing behind me.

Mr. Blair thanked me for my "kindness." I asked him to sign baseball, and he obliged. I remember that his smile widened: it seemed to become even more radiant. I contemplated asking him if I could call him Motormouth, but I refrained. So I asked him something else.

"You were teammates with Davey Johnson, right?"

"That's right. He was always smart. The Mets are lucky to have him as their manager."

"And now he's my boss," the man in front of Paul said.

Mr. Blair laughed. "That's right, Bud."

"Bud?"

"Where are my manners? Allow me to introduce my good friend and Davey's favorite Third Base Coach, Bud Harrelson. Bud, this is my man Joey."

The wind nearly shoved my eyes out of their sockets, but one last downpour poured out of my mouth.

"Holy crap. My father loves you," I said.

The three of us spoke for about 10 minutes. Only the Hills East hallway walls know the exact words of my sentences, but the general tenor of them were compiled of thanks and praise for all of the great memories they created for me and my family. I also recall saying something to the effect of how respected they were, that they were as revered as my Nonna Ida or Grandfather Joe. I tried not to be too effusive, but any efforts to suppress such tendencies would have been in vain. It had stopped raining outside, but there was a torrent of lavish praise pouring from my mouth.

Mr. Blair and Bud smiled and laughed the whole way through. Perhaps they had grown accustomed to being flattered by fans, and were simply performing a part of their job with the same ease in which they chased down fly balls or turned the double play. Even if they were indulging me, it didn't matter.

At one point, Motormouth turned to Bud. "This is why I love coming back to New York. The fans treat you like family here."

Bud nodded. My mouth gaped open in astonishment, knowing that two of the most beloved ballplayers my relatives and I rooted for returned the love that we gave them, as much as they could.

*   *   *

When I was 11 years old, my Grandmother Mary told me that my father was almost named Robert instead of Joseph. Not Roberto.

Not Bob or Bobby. Just Robert. She loved the Anglicized version of Roberto, because my father was an American native, and she wanted him to have a clear sense of who he was, rather than being thought of as another version of her husband, my Grandfather Joe.

Saying the name Robert made her "want to dance," just as seeing dirt or mud on my feet after playing outside drove her into a frenzy of panic. It was important to her that I wore shoes, as a reminder of the need to protect oneself from the unpredictability of the world, how the air could clench its "sooty hands into fists" and "knock you around." My father knew the fist-wind well, having had a family sooner than he originally planned. Grandmother Mary almost lost Grandfather Joe to the Nazis in World War Two, and was elated that his Sherman Tank didn't become "a mausoleum on wheels," so she complied with his directive to name my father Joseph Michael. The fist wind punched Grandfather Joe around, but he returned home and met my father three months after he was born.

A month or so after Grandmother Mary told me this story, I went through a phase of calling myself "Fred." I decided on it because I didn't know anyone personally with the name. In addition to all of the people with the names Joseph, Michael, variants on Anthony, Mary and Nicolo in my family—many of whom I lived under the same roof with—the sound of Fred was powdered sugar melting on my tongue after the first bite of a fresh zeppole. The name was also becoming on many famous people, such as the actors Fred Astaire, Fred Gywnne, and the slugging Boston Red Sox outfielder Fred Lynn, so I tried it on.

My father thought it was a poor fit. "Fred? As in Flintstone? You're my son, not a cartoon."

* * *

When I knew Grandfather Joe, his life was a parade of wisecracks, fishing, playing Bingo on Friday nights with Grandmother Mary, and watching TV. Among his favorite programs: New York Yankees baseball and New York Islanders hockey telecasts. I often watched TV with him in the comfort of his living room: he in a beige recliner, me on the left end of his navy blue and pink floral couch. My father joined us when he wasn't working, and sat at the other end of the couch.

Grandfather Joe was similar to Yogi Berra in that his predilection for malapropisms rarely failed to bring down the house or amuse himself. For instance, he called the Yankees outfielder Sweet Lou Piniella Lou "Sweet Lou Vanilla," the New York Islanders left winger John Tonelli "Johnny Torelli," and the Great One, the Edmonton Oilers Center Wayne Gretzky either "Gratzko" or my personal favorite, "The Great Gonzo." I wasn't sure as to whether or not he did this on purpose or if he simply couldn't remember their exact names of certain athletes, but it always made the game we were watching all the more enjoyable.

Then there were some names Grandfather Joe knew just fine. Perhaps the most memorable case in point was Jiggs McDonald, the former Islanders play-by-play announcer. A native of Ontario, Canada, Jiggs was born John Kenneth McDonald in Gait, and was the original voice of the NHL's Los Angeles Kings, who he called games for from 1967-1972. In addition to the Kings, Jiggs also called games for the Atlanta Flames from 1973 until their relocation to Calgary, Alberta at the conclusion of the 1979-80 season. He started broadcasting games for the Islanders in the 1980-81 season and continued to do so until 1995. Jiggs also called baseball games for the New York Mets during the 1982 season, which was the only year and reason why Grandfather Joe watched them regularly.

Each game became a spectacle about which player's name Grandfather Joe would change, not to mention his befuddled fascination with Mr. McDonald's inimitable nickname.

"Jiggs!?!? Hey Jiggs! You crazy guy! What's up with your name?" He'd say to his Mahogany Zenith set. "Hey Joefish," he 'd then ask me. "Where'd he get a name like Jiggs?" I'd usually shrug my shoulders, which always elicited the following response:

"Oh well. The jig's up. Ha!"

Maybe it's genetic, but my father and I also had baseball players who intrigued us because of their nicknames as much as their games. My father was a fan of Derrel McKinley "Bud" Harrelson, the former gold glove Mets shortstop who had begun coaching third base for them part way through the 1985 season. In addition to Motormouth,

My favorite Yankee players were Graig "Puff" Nettles, Ron Guidry, who was called "Gator" by his teammates—because he is a Louisiana native—and Louisiana Lightning by Phil "Scooter" Rizzuto, the former Yankees star shortstop and then-current broadcaster, Fred "Chicken" Stanley, Dick "Dirt" Tidrow, Reggie "Mr. October" Jackson, Albert "Sparky" Lyle, and former Yankees star and then-current coach, Yogi Berra among others.

The late 1970's Yankee teams were as known for their strong personalities as they were for their World Championships, which has become known as "The Bronx Zoo" era in franchise history. Of all of the players in this era, I was especially intrigued with Motormouth because he was a former all-star and gold glove outfielder with the Baltimore Orioles before he joined the Yankees in 1977. The Yankees used him primarily as a defensive replacement, and I couldn't get enough of watching him pick it in the field like a boss. I also dug on the nickname "Motormouth," which was reportedly given to him for his singular affability, his love of chatting it up with teammates, members of the media, fans, and strangers alike, the latter of which I was thrilled to have experienced first-hand.

Shakespeare's notion of "what's in a name" has always been at issue in my family. Both of my parents are named after theirs, just as my sister and I are named after ours. While this not so unusual in itself, I have been as interested in the thinking behind the decision making process that went into it for as long as I can remember, and my inquiries to my parents about what figured into my own name was often met with a similar confusion and amusement that Grandfather Joe had for Jiggs McDonald. I remember asking my mother how she and my father chose my name: was there a process? Were there other candidates beside Joseph? Was as I close to being named something else? Why was Joseph chosen for me, as opposed to Giuseppe? Why not Michael Joseph as opposed to the other way around? Why not Fred?

My mother didn't respond to my queries so much as she reacted to them, much like Grandfather Joe whenever he watched a hockey or ball game called by Jiggs. "That was always your father's top choice, and mine as well. We *planned* it that way."

Her emphasis on the word "planned" always seemed as if there was more behind it than was being said, though it's just as likely that the opposite was true. I have never found out for certain. What I have learned is that there was some talk about me possibly named Carmine, but it was just that. This made me ask why the name of Carmine never got past the talking stage. My mother's reply: "Go ask your father."

When I posed the question to my father, he rolled his eyes and first said the phrase that has since become a trademark in our conversations: "You gotta be different!"

My sense of being "different" is more to do with knowing myself and understanding all that figures into it, more than being unique for the sake of simply doing so. Wallace Stegner argued, "You can't know who are unless you know where you are." I was a teenaged boy with an inchoate understanding about what figured into who I was and how I got to Long Island, even though I was born in New York City. I was well aware of my Italian heritage, yet the only time I heard the language—or at least the Orsognese dialect of it—spoken was on special occasions, such as weddings, christenings, confirmations, wakes, funerals, or when my mother and Nonna Ida spoke to each other on the phone. Such occurrences did not happen every day. That they proceeded with a different tongue—one that I did not speak, at that—made them all the memorable in their pageantry, as well as in their reminder of what I didn't know about myself. I was always called "Giuseppe" on such occasions, and never "Joe," "Joefish," "Mojo" "JoJo," or any of the other names my family had for me. I also didn't feel the need to insist on being addressed as Fred or anything else, because it felt authentic to be called "Giuseppe," which is to say that it felt natural, and thus correct. I was being told part of my story without having asked about it. The jig was up.

So I had to be different. After my father coined this now Nicoletti-family favorite phrase, I gradually became less insistent on being called Fred. In my heart, I was Giuseppe. In my family's house, I was a variety of others, but "Joey" was an unclaimed suitcase in my home's verbal baggage claim, so I picked it up. Further, when I was with my closest friends, I was often addressed as "Joey," so I began to introduce myself as such. For all of the other variations of my name that my family members had for me, Joey became my favorite: the leader of the naming pack.

This excavation of what's in my name has yielded an unexpected find: professional sports has been an archeology of sorts, a study in which I have analyzed the details of my personal history and prehistory, where trading/bubblegum cards, autographed baseballs, VHS recorded games, magazine articles, newspaper clippings, books, and family photo albums have been my primary sources. Watching professional sports in person and on TV with my family, playing them with friends and foes has given me a fluency to connect with people that I might otherwise might not have had, even though there was more than one tongue spoken in my family. Names: nicknames account for a sizeable portion of my fondness for professional sports, which is an extension of the pride and fervor I have for my family and heritage. What Jiggs McDonald was to Grandfather Joe and Bud Harrelson was to my father, Paul Motormouth Blair was to me: a way of connecting, of considering what it meant or could mean to be a human being in the world, which in our case meant being men with interests as similar as our names and places of residence and descent, yet of different generations making their way in 1970's and 1980's New York City and Long Island, where the three of us spent a significant amount of time together.

*   *   *

"You're on, Bud," the steel wool-haired teenager said. "10 more minutes, Mr. Blair."

Bud waved good-bye and stepped into the backstage area. Mr. Blair took removed a sheet of paper from a pocket inside his sports jacket, and I listened: the beginning of Stevie Wonder's song "I Just Called to Say I Love You" echoed in the hallway, and Jiggs' introduction of Bud thundered through the Hills East All-Purpose Room.

Mr. Blair put his sheet of paper back into his pocket, and we chatted for a few more minutes. In other words, he spoke, and I hung on every word. He told me about how much he enjoyed his time with the Yankees. He paused for a moment, and I no longer heard rain or wind.

The teenager appeared again, like the sun outside the window. "Hello, Mr. Goring. You'll be on later."

I looked behind me: the man with the receding hairline was none other than Butch Goring himself. I gasped.

"Wow. What's up, Mr. Goring?"

Mr. Goring smiled. "I'm doing okay, son. Did I hear you introduce yourself to Paul and Bud as *Jerry?*"

I laughed. "Joey."

Before Mr. Goring could reply, I had pulled out my picture of him and asked him to sign it. "Sure. As long as you call me Butch," he said.

Then the teenager appeared again, like the sun outside the window. I shook hands with Butch and Mr. Blair, and they followed the teenager backstage.

I walked down the hall and found the auditorium entrance, where I was trying to get to in the first place. The doors were unlocked. I grabbed a seat towards the back row, during the last part of Bud's talk.

Jiggs thanked Bud, and I scanned the crowd. I recall that there were few empty seats, and that there were more women than men in attendance. The women were of all ages, predominantly teenagers or young mothers. This was most likely due to the upcoming appearance of Pat LaFontaine, who was the Islanders' current heartthrob, and whose talk would conclude the event.

The beginning of Paul's talk marked the beginning of an awful headache, which worsened when Butch spoke, so I don't remember exactly what they said or how they said it.

However, when Jiggs announced Pat, women and girls screamed and hollered: it was as if Pat was one of the Beatles. Only the fathers and Islander fans applauded, which continued on for a minute or so.

Pat somehow managed to deliver his speech, but the combination of my headache and all of the screaming made it difficult for me to make out what he said. I can only recall the gist of his talk, which was "Think before you act." Being the featured speaker, his talk ran longer than all of the others, going on for 15 minutes.

When Pat finished, the audience was louder than they previously were, giving him a standing ovation, as if he just scored the game-winning goal in game seven of the Stanley Cup finals. Bud and Butch sat in their chairs onstage, nodding and applauding, as did Mr. Blair, his radiant smile nearly blinding me. I was convinced that there would be no further rain that day.

Jiggs gave a few obligatory words of thanks to all of the participants in "today's important talk," and told everyone to get home safely. I grabbed my knapsack to go, my head throbbing, with the opening notes of "I Just Called . . . " echoing in my brain.

Then the teenaged boy and a silver-haired man in a plaid sports jacket directed the crowd to the front exits of the auditorium. I followed the flow of the crowd. When I got close to the stage right auditorium exit, a group of teenaged girls and boys clad in blue and white Pat LaFontaine jerseys stormed the stage. There were about ten of them: one of them shoved me, and I got caught in the undertow of and polyester and cotton wave, which eventually crashed on the stage.

When I finally separated myself from the crowd, I watched them chase Pat to the backstage area. Then I saw Jiggs, who was about two feet in front of me. He shook someone's hand, and then did a double take as he saw me knotting the top laces of each of high tops.

"Young man," he said in his perfect broadcaster's cadence. "What are you doing here?"

The jig was up. "Putting shoes on, Jiggs," I replied. "Gotta run."

Jiggs looked baffled, which was my cue to run down the stage steps and exit to the left. I recall being surprised at how many members of the audience were scattered in the hallway, hoping to catch a sight of Pat, or any of the other speakers. I could only imagine how they must have felt, given that they were probably tired and did not desire to be mobbed or besotted with autograph requests. I put my head down and began to search for the nearest bathroom.

The lobby phone area was as close as I got. I unzipped my bag: everything was present and accounted for. Then, checking my laces, I sauntered past the burly security guard, who was taking a drag of his smoke. I sniffed the air, coughed, and then scanned the sun-splotched parking lot for my father's car.

Assassin's Hours

All I wanted was a date for Friday night.

By the time I was 15, my family and I had moved to a community where every house was two stories high, had bay windows, potted begonias on the front porches, and occupants who preferred hockey to baseball. I didn't know what accounted for my new neighborhood's sports partiality, but I was certain that I wanted to get with the shapely, sophisticated girls who lived on the aptly named Honey Lane. I was also disconcerted that my Graig Nettles Louisville Slugger was being used less and less, even though there was a path across the street that went directly to the baseball field at my brother's new elementary school.

This is not to say that I disliked hockey. In fact, I enjoyed it quite a bit. I followed the NHL, and the New York Islanders were my favorite team. Not only had they won four consecutive Stanley Cup championships, they were also the first American-based franchise to do so, and only the second team in NHL history to achieve the feat.

The early 1980's were an opportune time to be a fan of New York Islanders hockey. My family's previous Teed Street digs was located just a few blocks away from the Islander defenseman Stefan Persson's hockey-season home. I had seen Jean Potvin, another Islander defenseman, in church on Sundays during the NHL off-season. I went to school with Stefan's daughter, and Jean always said hello to me and my family. In addition to being the best at what they did, many of the Islander players and their families were my neighbors and affable human beings, so I couldn't help but root for them.

When I played hockey, I imagined myself as John Tonelli, the Islanders' All-Star left wing, who was my favorite player. In addition to being of Italian descent, I admired John's game, particularly his tenacity on the boards and for his relentless pursuit of the puck, especially if it involved digging it out of the corners of Nassau Coliseum or any other NHL arena. What's more, he also had terrific passing ability and a knack for scoring clutch goals. In thinking about it now, the combination of John's work ethic, wavy jet-black hair, and sinewy build, was a personification of the full-grown adult I wanted to become: strong, diligent, and persistent, performing at his best when it was most needed.

I didn't know how to ice or roller skate, so I played deck hockey. I didn't have a particularly strong or accurate shot, but I was a hustler. I crashed the corners of junior high school gymnasiums or cracked sidewalks to come up with the puck or ball, determined to do whatever was needed to help my team prosper.

In so doing, I thought that knowing a little bit about the sport would help me adjust to my new surroundings and make some friends. I didn't fail and I didn't succeed.

Perhaps the best example of this could be seen in the case of my neighbor Chad, who lived across the street. He was also 15, stood nearly six feet tall, and was a rabid New York Rangers fan, which in his case meant that the Islanders were the team he hated more than anything else in "the known universe," as he was wont to say.

"John Tonelli's a pussy," Chad said. "Nicky Boy would whip his Islander ass in front of the known universe."

"Nicky Boy" referred to Nick Fotiu, the New York Rangers' hard-checking left wing. A Staten Island native and former Golden Gloves boxer, Nicky had an Italian mother. Combined with his willingness to toss pucks up to the crowd after pre-game warm-ups, he was a Rangers fan favorite. His number 22 jerseys can still be seen in Madison Square Garden, MSG, the Rangers' home arena, particularly in the blue seats, the nosebleed section, which Chad referred to as "Real Fan Land."

I admired Nicky Boy's game almost as much as John's, but I didn't tell Chad. As a pubescent Islander fan, I felt compelled to despise all Rangers, even if they had Italian bloodlines or New York roots, and especially if a player had an important role with them, as Nicky Boy did, so I changed the topic to football and asked him about his preferences.

"J-E-T-S," Chad said, recalling the cheer of Jets fans during their home games. "You?"

"Seattle Seahawks. Gotta love Steve Largent."

"Strike three," Chad said. "What are ya, crazy? Seahawks aren't actual birds, and the Islanders blow goats. Sayonara, Sweetheart."

I thought that this would be our last conversation. But in the weeks that followed, we played a lot of deck hockey, either in the middle of Honey Lane or in Chad's driveway. He had two nets and enough sticks, replacement blades, helmets, and pairs of gloves for those who needed them, which was rarely the case.

Chad and I played with as many as 20 people some days, where the white garage door of his family's house was dented and scuffed with errant slap shots. Eddie Junior, Chad's older brother, called our games "Assassin's Hours." To our hockey sticks, every sound was an electric guitar arpeggio, a Moog synthesizer hum or whoosh from the music of Tears for Fears.

I was one of the shorter kids on the block, most of whom were older, had mullets, and wore Swatches. They were also Ranger fans, and they did not want to lose on account of an Islander fan, especially one who was an outsider, or "Baby Tonelli," as Eddie Junior had dubbed me, so we played chippy games. I dug the puck out of the corners. I didn't instigate fights or back down from them. I checked. I got knocked on my ever-loving Baby Tonelli ass and got right back up. Tears for Fears encouraged me to shout and let it all out, so I did.

One game was especially joyous. I dug the ball out of a corner and made a quick pass to Chad, who slapped it over Kyle Tanner's right shoulder to for the victory. Kyle was Chad's homeboy and the team captain of our high school's varsity Ice Hockey team, which never won more than four games during his three-year tenure as the leader of the Ice Tigers, as I referred to them. Sayonara, Sweetheart.

Then Chad invited me inside his house. The foyer was lined with photos of his family members on one side, and Ranger players on the other, all of which were in color, autographed, and encased in shiny gold frames.

Their picture of Nicky Boy caught my eye. He was punching an unidentified opponent, his fist covering the player's face, blood on his knuckles.

We were greeted in the kitchen by a short dog with tall brown ears and spots all over its white coat.

"Hi there," I said. "What's your name?"

"This is Ranger. Right, you little bastard?"

Ranger snarled at Chad, who flashed a self-satisfied smirk.

"Whatsamatta, Ranger? Are you a pussy?"

I scratched the back of Ranger's ears. Chad raised an eyebrow.

"Poor Ranger. Poor, poor doggie. Poor, poor non-cat, pussy bastard doggie."

Ranger growled and barked. Chad burst out laughing and winked at me.

"Fuhgedaboutit. Ranger's pissed cuz' he has no mother."

Ranger's growl grew louder. Chad cleared his throat, and began to chant:

> *Ranger has no mo-ther.*
> *Ranger has no mo-ther.*
> *Ranger has no mo-ther.*

I noticed that Ranger's whip-like tail had stopped wagging. Then Eddie Junior came into the kitchen and joined in:

> *Ranger has no mo-ther.*
> *Ranger has no mo-ther.*
> *Ranger has no mo-ther.*

Within a minute or so, Amanda, Chad and Eddie Junior's baby sister, and Mr. Ed, their father, joined the chant. They formed a semicircle around Ranger, and gradually increased the chant's tempo, which evolved into a loud crescendo:

> *Ran-ger has no mo-ther.*
> *Ran-ger has no mo-ther.*
> *Ran-ger has no mo-ther.*

Ranger growled and barked the marble off of the countertops. Then he snapped at Chad's hand. I wanted to leave my gear in the driveway and take Ranger home with me instead.

The doorbell rang. It's tinny "ding-dong" made Mr. Ed leave the circle. Dinner had arrived. 10 pizzas. The semicircle and the chant broke down, and Ranger ran through the open sliding door in the living room and took refuge in his house, which was behind the diving board of the in-ground pool, streaked with soot and grime.

Mr. Ed put the pizza boxes on the kitchen island and smiled at me. "You hungry, Joe? I dunno about you, but all this fun has built up my appetite."

"No thanks," I said. "My Mom's making baked ziti tonight."

"Aha. She certainly knows her way around ziti," Mr. Ed said. Then he winked at me.

"Yeah. Thanks again."

I grabbed my gear. The sky was lavender and I was morose.

*   *   *

Chad and I never became close. We acknowledged each other's presence in our junior high and high school hallways with a nod or the occasional verbal exchange of "What's up," but little else.

This disappointed my mother. She attributed our disinterest in each other's friendship to Chad and I not knowing each other well.

I can't say for sure whether or not she was right. All I am certain of is that when I was 15, my interests were girls, music, sports, comics, pizza, and girls. My high school, my new school, was noted for its music program, particularly its marching band, which was open to any student who was interested in it, and was compiled of 300 people.

Even better, nearly 200 of the band members were girls; almost 260 if you counted the kick and flag line squads. Seeing as how I had played the trumpet in my previous middle school band, I figured that it would be a sage move to join: the odds of getting a date were too good for me to pass up. I became a member of the Tiger Marching Band in my sophomore year.

One Friday night I went to an Ice Tigers hockey game with some of my new band friends. One of them was a flute player named Sarah Posh, who had the longest, the most flaxen hair and mesmerizing sapphire eyes I had ever seen. Sarah was a sophomore, one grade ahead of me and a fervent hockey fan, especially of the Rangers.

Tears for Fears' "Head over Heels" boomed through the arena. Roland Orzabal sang about the hardships of being a man with a gun in your hand. Sarah turned to me and pointed toward the ice.

"Look! Here come our guys. Don't they just warm your jets?"

"Mmm, Jets. J-E-T-S."

"What?"

"Mmm."

Then the Ice Tigers came out for their pre-game skate. Kyle, who waved and blew kisses to the crowd, led them.

Chad skated towards the penalty box area of the stands. Some of my friends called out his name. We made eye contact for a moment, which he acknowledged with his trademark smirk. Then his smirk widened into a toothy smile when he spotted Sarah, her leather-lunged cheers scratching their way into the dimly lit arena ice.

Other Plans

When I was a child, my mother informed me that I needed a new winter jacket and that I was going to get one for Christmas.

I asked if I could get a Death Star play set instead. My mother dashed that hope, saying that Santa Claus had "other plans," which was why we had the Wish Book, a catalogue that the Sears and Roebuck Company put out every year during the holiday shopping season when I was a child.

The silver lining to my cloud of disappointment was that I could pick the jacket I wanted from the Wish Book. Perhaps the force was with me more than I realized. With my mother looking over my shoulder, I chose a jacket with the colors and emblem of the Seattle Seahawks: my favorite NFL franchise.

"The Seahawks?" my father asked. "We're Jets fans in this house. Talk some sense into your son, Marie."

"Oh, Joe," my mother said. "Joefish needs a jacket. Let him choose what he wants. It's Christmas time, after all."

My father sighed. "Ya know what I want? I want a beer. And steak. But I'll start with the beer since there's no steak in this household."

"Household?" my mother asked. "Do you see any silos in our back yard? Grab a Schaefer and a seat, man. You're making my ears bleed."

"Just one question, Joefish. Why the Seahawks?"

I explained that I was a fan of their star players: Jim Zorn, the team's original starting quarterback, and Steve Largent, the team's All-Pro wide receiver, both of whom I had seen play on TV. Jim was a dynamic presence on the field, due to his scrambling ability and his strong throwing arm, which he often used to connect with Steve. Steve was quick, ran flawless routes, and never seemed to drop a pass.

I also chose the Seahawks to defy my father. As much as I have always enjoyed professional sports, he always felt the need to tell me why I should or shouldn't like a particular team or player, which often came out in the phrase, "You gotta be different."

He also used this phrase to express his exasperation with me in other subjects or situations, including my Seahawks jacket. This was unusual, because he usually left clothing matters to my mother. But now that sports figured into the equation, he gave his opinion, not that anyone had asked for it.

"The Seahawks play in Seattle. We live in New York."

"Golly, that's a sophisticated argument, Joe," my mother said. "All hail Mr. Geography."

My father took a sip of his beer. "Honestly, Joefish. You gotta be different."

The jacket was spectacular. It was mostly sky blue, and had a hood with sea green fur, and a thick, glossy silver zipper ran down the middle: it was like having an unbreakable, portable mirror in a jacket. Surely no bad luck would be had. The interior of the jacket also had sea-green fur. There was a rectangular patch on the back with "Seahawks" stitched in silver with green trimming. What's more, there was a round patch on the front left side of the jacket, which had the words, "Seattle Seahawks" stitched in green lettering above the team helmet.

The patch was my favorite part of the jacket, because I was taken with the team emblem: the silver helmet, the Sea green and Sky blue condor, staring straight ahead, looking as if it was going to peck someone's eyes out. The Seahawk emblem looked the way I felt when I was ensnared in a situation beyond my control. Like being chastised for having a preference for skyscrapers to tract housing.

My Seahawks jacket also had the virtue of not being owned by anyone else back home on Teed Street. I found it to be an apt flag of my individuality in the wool jungle of Kelly green and white New York Jets hats at my bus stop and elementary school playground. Thus, I made my choice. Go Hawks.

My birthday is in January, so as only child reasoning could dictate, I thought that since I had cooperated with my parents, perhaps they could do the same for me. When they asked me what I wanted for my birthday, I said that I wanted to go to a Seahawks game at the Kingdome, the Seahawks' former digs.

My father furrowed his eyebrow. "You mean in Seattle?" That's all the way across the country, Joefish," he said. "We'd have to fly to get there."

"Sounds good to me," I said.

"I dunno," he said. "We'll have to see. Besides, do they have good pizza out there? I dunno."

*   *   *

I saw the Seahawks play at Giants Stadium 5 years later. This was the closest I ever got to the Kingdome, the Seahawks' original home arena, which was demolished in 2000. My father had gotten tickets from a co-worker, who was a Jets season ticket holder. The Jets had just relocated to Giants Stadium, the former home of the New York Football Giants, from playing their home games at Shea Stadium the year before. If I couldn't go to Seattle, it was worth enduring traffic on the New Jersey Turnpike and my father blasting his infernal Dion and the Belmonts mixtapes on his Blapunkt tape deck to watch Steve Largent and his teammates play some American football. I was ecstatic. I slept for only a few hours the night before the game, and I did so wearing my Seahawks baseball cap and Steve Largent jersey.

Unfortunately, I had grown in the past 5 years; my family and I moved to a town closer to Long Island Sound, and Jim Zorn was no longer a member of the Seahawks.

Even so, I had gotten a new Seahawks jacket during the previous winter, which I wore to the game. As was the case with my first Seahawks jacket, my new one was a sight to behold. It was hoodless and had a high school letterman type of design. The team name wasn't stitched on the back like it was on my previous jacket, but the sleeves were silver, and the front and back were Sky blue. The patch with the team name and helmet was on the left side, but there were green buttons instead of a zipper, which was a cool variation. Rarely have I enjoyed what I wore as much as I did when I was dressed in my Seahawks jackets or jerseys. My Seahawks gear was on point; I felt as if I was an official member of the 12th man: The 12's, the name of the Seahawks fan base, and I was proud of it. Unabashedly.

To be part of the 12's was to think for myself. While my family wasn't poor in the greater sense of the word, we were in the context of our new town. The overwhelming majority of my new peers had parents who were college graduates, had six-figure salaries, some of whom had professional ties to the Jets, including one person whose father was the team's primary physician, and another whose father was an assistant coach. These and other classmates had been training for similar careers since they were children. Some were legacies: these people had elitist attitudes towards anyone who wasn't in their parents' tax bracket. They knew they were going to über-exclusive universities and colleges such as Princeton, Williams, or Dartmouth, no matter what they did or didn't accomplish, like their parents, grandparents, and great-grandparents before them, with their sights set on finding a new cul de sac and staying there for the rest of their lives. They swaggered down immaculate school hallways and lamppost-lit streets; from high-end store to high-end store in the gleam of shopping malls, wallets and purses swollen with their parents' cash and credit cards, knowing they would never be held accountable for any legal or social transgression, and their smarmy tones of voice poured in bile yellow light out of hallway skylights and windows as they strutted to and from their pristine ivy-green lockers.

I didn't know precisely what I wanted out of life in my junior high: middle school years, but I was certain that I wanted to see as much of the world as I could. I had yet to visit Seattle or taste its pizza, but the players of its NFL franchise encouraged me to feel comfortable in my own skin, more than some people in both, my new neighborhood and my own family ever did. For my parents, Long Island was their land of independence, the place in the world where they established themselves as diligent, responsible adults. They felt that had to leave an urban environment to do so, the cultural and financial hurdles be damned. Looking back, I began to think that Seattle would be to me what Long Island was to them. I, too, had other plans. Begin seeing the rest of the world by going west, I thought. Go Hawks.

* * *

About a month or so later, my father began to check in with me weekly, by asking me about "life in the semi-city." While I appreciated the fact that my father was trying to talk with me, it felt more like he was talking *at* me. He took great pride in working long hours and residing in a neighborhood that was leafier than our previous one, so much so that he wanted me to like it as much as he did. His talks were a sales pitch gone berserk, and I wasn't buying. I couldn't afford it.

"Hey! Joefish! How's life in the semi-city? How's school goin'?"

"Ok, Pops."

"Ok? Whaddya mean, 'Ok?'"

"Well, there are some kids whose parents give them Benjamins for lunch money."

"So?"

"Brown bag lunches are basically frowned upon."

"So we have rich neighbors. What's wrong with that?"

"It's not the money," I said. "It's the attitude of some of the people who have it. It sucks and I don't like it."

My father sighed. "Man, Joefish. You're the only guy I know who would see having too much money as a problem."

"I just don't think it's the beginning and end of the world," I said. "I know I need it, but—"

"No buts. If you got no money, you got no car, no house. Or a family to fill it. Ya want a family, right? To do that, ya gotta have a woman, a wife, to make a family with, and that'll cost ya something extra. Ya gotta wine and dine her for that to happen. Food, especially fancy, let's get naked together-food costs money. There ain't no point yearnin' if you ain't earnin', Joefish. Remember that."

"What if I don't want a house?" I asked. What if I want to live somewhere else? Someplace other than Long Island?"

My father smirked. "Like where? Denver? San Francisco? Maybe Seattle. Every Seahawks game would be on TV."

I felt the sun rise in my chest. After all of our talks, some of what I said had stuck with my father. I felt triumphant, as if I had invented the world's first time machine.

"That's right," I said. "You understand, don't you, Pop?"

My father shook his head. "Yeah. I understand just fine. My grammar ain't too good, but I know that you gotta be different."

* * *

Steve caught only two passes in the game, but it didn't keep me from shouting his name at the top of my voice or waving my Seahawks pennant every chance I had. This was not appreciated by some of the Jets fans I sat with, including the burly, middle-aged man who informed me of his disapproval with vociferous panache in the fourth quarter, when Wesley Walker, the Jets' All-Pro Wide Receiver, scored the game-winning touchdown.

"Let's see you wave that Seahawk banner now," he yelled. My face felt like a target sheet at a shooting range, being pelted with bullets of spit, potato chip crumbs, and droplets of stale beer.

I held my banner over my head. "Go Hawks," I said.

Burly Jet Fan rolled his blood-shot eyes. "Fuck that and fuck you, you little Seahawks shit," he said. "The Jets are goin' all the way this year!"

"Unlike you and your old lady," I said.

My father slapped the back of my head. "Joefish!"

"Thanks Man," Burly Jet Fan said to my father.

My father nodded his head. "Let's go," he said. "Traffic's gonna bite the big one."

"Not as bad as the Seahawks did today," Burly Jet Fan said. "J-E-T-S. Jets, Jets, Jets," he and a few other ruddy-faced fans clad in Jets jerseys yelled as we made our way down the aisle.

"Fuck a duck," my father said. "You gotta be different."

My father's thoughts about traffic biting the big one were prescient. The way he saw it, we would be on the road for nearly three hours for a trip that should only be just over an hour's drive. We would miss dinner, which gave him an idea.

When we crossed back into New York, we had a nosh at a pizzeria somewhere on Utopia Parkway. We talked about the game over a meal of garlic knots, Coca-Cola, a Sicilian pie and lemon Italian ices. Our discussion was a concert of sorts: my father singing the praises of Wesley Walker and our pizza; me of Steve Largent; of wishing that Jim Zorn would have been under center for the Seahawks instead of holding a clipboard for the Green Bay Packers; Dion and the Belmonts wondering why loud and clear on the jukebox.

Going to Fishbein's

Superheroes don't need capes.

Whenever my family and I visited my Nonna Ida, she often sent me to pick up milk, bread, and other assorted items she needed from Fishbein's, a convenience store that was two blocks away from her apartment in Astoria, Queens, New York City. Her arthritis had made it difficult for her to walk, so it became my unofficial job to get her whatever she needed for Sunday dinner or her meals for the rest of the week.

Nonna Ida also wanted me to enjoy every possible moment of my visit. To this point, it was standard practice for her to give me twenty dollars to pick up whatever she needed from Fishbein's, even though her bill often amounted to ten dollars or less. She did this to be sure that I had spending money. "You buy something," she said. "You young. Now da time to have good time."

In addition to having an extensive refrigerated section and several aisles of perishable food items, Fishbein's was also memorable to me for its front entrance, which had a Space Invaders video arcade game and two racks of comic books, which were available for purchase. All of the most recent issues of mainstream comics were arranged in alphabetical order on both racks; spinning and looking through them made me dizzy with joy.

This would be my first order of business when I was sent to Fishbein's. At a time when new comics could be purchased for 35 to 50 cents and before I was eligible to work or was aware of direct-only stores or comic shops, I was thrilled about the opportunity to buy multiple comics in the same place, which had been afforded to me by Nonna Ida's generosity and the proximity of her home to my favorite childhood hangout. So I scoured the racks, picked out a few comics, and asked whoever was working the cash register if they would put them aside for me while I shopped. This request was never denied. The people of Fishbein's were as dope as their merchandise.

My favorite trip to Fishbein's took place in March of 1979, when I scored a copy of *The Amazing Spider Man:* ASM issue 190, which was titled, "In Search of the Man-Wolf." Spider-Man: "Spidey" was my favorite superhero, largely because of his alter ego, Peter Parker. For all of Peter's intelligence and abilities, such as climbing walls and his Spider Sense, which warned him of danger being nearby, he shrank his Spidey costume in the wash, was often late for classes, lived from paycheck to paycheck, and was unlucky in love. I didn't always have access to buying comics on my own, so I was especially excited about the chance to do so on this particular day.

ASM issue 190 features Man-Wolf, an old nemesis of Spidey's, whose alter ego was John Jameson, a former NASA Astronaut, who has kidnapped his father, J. Jonah Jameson. Jonah is the irritable Editor-in-Chief of the Daily Bugle, the newspaper that buys Peter's photographs more than any other in New York City.

Spidey chases after Man-Wolf and catches up with him and Jonah on the Brooklyn Bridge, where they fight. Jonah is saved, and the Man-Wolf changes back into John, who then falls off the bridge. Spidey shoots a web to try and catch John before he hits the water, but he vanishes just before the web reaches him.

Spidey and Jonah are stunned. Jonah accuses Spidey of being a murderer, and the issue ends with both men staring in different directions, rain pounding down on them.

I gathered Nonna Ida's items and purchased them along with my comic in record time. I strutted out the door, as if I was John Travolta, carrying cans of paint in the opening scenes of the movie *Saturday Night Fever*, instead of groceries and my book. My breath drifted and twisted in the funky city air, like the newspaper pages and Canary-yellow fast food wrappers poked by the wind as I made my way back to the apartment.

"So, Giuseppe," Nonna Ida said. "You buy books of da people in da bright underwear?"

"Yes, Nonna."

I took my comic out of the bag. Nonna Ida studied the cover carefully. "Ah. Da Spider Man. He no have a cape, just like you no have change, si?"

"Si, Nonna."

"Ok," Nonna Ida said. "You read now. Enjoy."

I planted myself in Nonna Ida's pumpkin orange love seat, which was beside her kitchen window. The window offered a marvelous view of the Triborough Bridge, which has been officially known as the Robert F. Kennedy Bridge since 2008. Nevertheless, it will always be known as The Triborough to me.

The Triborough is my heart's and mind's foremost bridge. This is due to the countless times I traveled on it and its relatively close proximity to Nonna Ida's apartment. When I rode beneath it with my family as a child, I was fascinated by the tall, sinewy teenagers who played basketball beneath it. I spent many an hour gazing at the Triborough from the window, jeweled with green and red lights at night, as if it was a steel and concrete Christmas tree, my belly filled with pasta and Nonna's sauce.

Like the vehicles on the bridge, my thoughts sped to the Bronx and Queens, the New York City boroughs I knew best. When we were in the neighborhood, my family bought soppressata, prosciutto, capicola, gnocchi, semolina bread, cannoli, and other assorted foods and imported Italian goods from butchers and shops on Arthur Avenue and Steinway Street. This made going to Fishbein's all the more joyous, because it was the first and only place that I was allowed to go to by myself in New York City when I was a child.

Then I shuffled back into the pumpkin orange love seat and gave my Spidey comic another read. In addition to enjoying the soap opera-esque plot and John Byrne's art again, I found myself paying closer attention to the script: the diction chosen by Marv Wolfman, whose surname made me laugh, given ASM issue 190's antagonist.

The last pieces of dialogue were especially striking. Jonah's last line was, "Leave me alone!" Spidey's was "But . . . but . . . ."

Many of the comics I read prior to this one ended with the usual genre stock phrase, such as, "Crime doesn't pay." This is not to say that I didn't enjoy such comics. After all, they were written for teen and tween readers, so their stories were designed to meet appropriate standards of style and content. To my understanding, comic books were meant to be fun, aspiring to stir their target audience's imagination and make serious bank.

Not only did ASM issue 190 succeed on these levels, it also transcended them, because it gave me a new idea of what heroism was or could be. Spidey's loss for words, presented him as vulnerable, just as my mother and nonni were when they came to America, and it was okay. It was not only permissible not to have all of the answers, it was perfectly fine to demonstrate or not have the initial means to articulate was—or wasn't the case. Even for people who were intelligent, fluent in their native tongue, other forms of communication, could climb walls, or sense danger before it happened.

In my life, no one epitomizes heroism more than Nonna Ida. Her determination and fortitude matched her boundless capacity for affection. She worked 6 days a week for nearly 40 years after she migrated to America, often taking multiple buses to and from her factory job at Drake's Baking Company. After going to mass, she spent the better part of her Sunday mornings walking throughout Astoria to purchase extra groceries, impervious to fatigue and the pain caused by her arthritis, shooting through her legs and feet. It was all so she and my family could have a nice dinner together.

That Nonna Ida trusted me to run errands for her was always a source of pleasure and pride. But in thinking about it now, it is much more than this. Even though I was born in Astoria, years passed before I saw enough of it to have a complete feel for the neighborhood's vitality. It was another country, a sort of inverse of my nonni's and mother's respective experiences in assimilating from Italian to Italian American. Astoria was my New World, and it was exotic, vibrant, and full of diversity and allure. The Triborough bridged the gap between the world I knew and the one I was eager to know; its vehicles came and went across the East River with astonishing speed from moment to moment, like Spidey in the moist panels of ASM issue 190.

*　*　*

Fishbein's has since closed and is now a mosque. Nonna Ida died almost two years after she moved out of Astoria. She was interred at St. Michael's, one of the oldest cemeteries in New York City. Even in death, she considered Queens her home, as opposed to Orsogna, Italy, where she was born and raised.

After her funeral, the car I was riding in stopped in front of her old building. I looked at the kitchen window. I thought of all the comics I had read there, most of which were purchased at Fishbein's, where people were now engaged in prayer, hands and faces on a rug as ornate as Spidey's costume; rain pounding the Triborough like a marimba.

Ducks and Geese

At the time, my partner Beth and I had a pond in our back yard. This was when we lived in Northeast Ohio. The pond froze over during the winter, but it was a veritable wet parkway for geese by the end of May, which drove Casey, our normally happy-go-lucky Boston terrier, bonkers. Even if he was rolling in mud or sniffing the grass at the edge of the yard, the sight of geese sent him into a frenzy, to the point where he would chase them back into the water, barking until they were out of sight, or better still, on the preserve in the middle of the pond.

One particular occurrence stands out. It was unseasonably sunny and warm outside, about 50 degrees or so. Casey was in the yard, prancing, running, rolling, and barking to his heart's content.

About 15 minutes passed where I didn't see or hear him. I checked the yard and noticed that the back door to the basement was opened, so I went inside, thinking that he might be there.

No such luck. I went upstairs and got the same results. I asked Beth, who was putting on her makeup, if she had seen Casey. She hadn't.

We went into the yard and searched. Casey was nowhere to be found. The prospect of losing him began to scare the bejesus out of me.

Then Beth looked out the bathroom window, where she caught a glimpse of his head.

She called after him. "Casey! What are you doing?"

He didn't hear her, which was astonishing, given the largeness of his ears. He was in the pond, about ten feet away from our backyard's shoreline, frantically paddling towards a brace of ducks, some of whom had turned around towards him. A pair of geese hissed in the distance, as if providing analysis and play-by-play commentary.

We ran to the shoreline. "Well, at least we know where he is," Beth said.

"And that he can swim," I replied. "I had no idea."

"Maybe he can swim us to our jobs. We'll save money on gas."

Beth's point was well taken. Nevertheless, this was no time to be concerned about work. I stripped down to my boxers and jumped into the pond. The water was colder than I expected, but Casey paddled vigorously and the geese hissed the sun into a cloud.

By the time I reached him, he was on the preserve. Some ducks and geese pecked at his face, and he responded by nipping at their legs. It's a wonder that his eyes were still in their sockets.

I grabbed him and put him in a headlock of sorts. He snarled at me, and twisted and turned his small, compact body every which way he could to remove himself from my grip. I almost let him go, because I was amazed at how awful he smelled: he reeked of a lethal combination of stagnant water and geese feces. As god is my witness, the putrid smell I caught a whiff of that day would serve any country well as a weapon of mass destruction in biochemical warfare. The Casey Bomb.

When we returned home, I took the longest shower of my life. Casey enjoyed a bath in the kitchen sink and a second breakfast of Milk Bone cookies.

Once I slipped into my bathrobe, Beth informed me that my sister Nicole had called and left a message. It was urgent.

I returned the call. Nicole informed me that our Nonna Ida, our mother's mother, had died after a six-month bout with cancer. Nicole had already begun wake and funeral arrangements and was hopeful that Beth and I could be in New York City by the end of the week.

*　*　*

As despondent as the moods of the wake and funeral were, my spirits lifted, as if reaching my backyard shoreline, when my father showed up on the last day Nonna Ida's body was viewed. Although my parents had been divorced for over two decades, my father had kept in touch with Nonna Ida, going so far as to visit her in the hospital during her final days. I was kneeling by her casket, in silent prayer when I became alerted to my father's presence.

"Hey! Joe," my Uncle Antonio, my Godfather shouted. "So glad you're here!"

"Hey! A-man," my father said. "A rosary for your thoughts. Is anyone else *dying* for pizza?"

The room erupted in laughter. Most of the visitors flocked towards my father, who was on the opposite side of the room. I made the sign of the cross, and joined the migration.

"Hi, Dad. I'm—"

"Surprised? Fuhgeddaboudit. I'm here to support you, your sister, and your brother."

"No way."

"Yeah way, Joefish. Whatever you need. Fuhgeddaboudit."

Uncle Antonio put his hand on my father's shoulder. "Hey! Joe!" Remember the time you used the bug lamp as a kite?"

"Hell if I know, A-man. All I remember was that I had as many strong drinks as my wife had strong words for me that night. Ha!"

* * *

Nonna Ida's funeral drained me. I was too depressed to talk to the Nicoletti side of the family. About six months passed before I did so. My father broke the silence with phone calls to Nicole and me, suggesting that we all go to a Long Island Ducks baseball game together, so that we can enjoy being a family again. I remember choking on a tortilla chip when he made this proposal; my lips stained with cheap red wine.

"The Ducks?" I asked. "Why not the Yankees? Or the Metsies?"

"Because I said so. Because the Ducks' stadium is around the corner from my house, because fuck traffic and because it's my fuckin' idea, and that's how it's gonna be. Capisce?"

I asked if I should purchase tickets beforehand. "Don't worry," he said. "I know a guy. We'll have enough for the whole family."

By "the whole family," my father meant that in addition to Beth, himself, and me, he'd get tickets for Nicole, her husband Tony, and their children Nino, JoJo, and Nicky.

"I can't get one for Casey, though. He's too small for the seats."

* * *

On the day we were supposed to go to the game, my father informed my sister that he wouldn't be able to make it, and that he wasn't able to get tickets, citing "an unavoidable change in plans" as the reason. He didn't elaborate.

I was annoyed, but Nicole took it in stride. "It's no big deal," She said quietly as she hung up the phone. "I'll stay home with Nicky. He's not feeling too good anyhow."

"That sucks," I said.

"It's no big deal. You, Beth, Nino, JoJo, and Tony can go."

"Will tickets be available?"

"Don't worry Joey," Tony said. "I know a guy."

Tony explained. He had a friend who had season tickets for the Ducks. Even better, one of the best perks of being season ticket holder gave him and his family access to have free food before games. The food came in the form of a buffet, which was compiled of all kinds of sustenance, which he had described as "world-class."

He walked out of the room, and made the call.

"Yeah. Yeah. Yeah? Yeah! All right. Great. Thanks, man."

I never heard Tony address his friend by name, but he referred to him as "My guy." As chance would have it, My Guy was out of town, so Tony could "help himself to his tickets." All we had to do was ask for them at the Will Call booth when we arrived at the ballpark.

Such matters are of great importance to the men of my family. To know a guy is to gain a leg up and it can reap many benefits, such as tickets to a ballgame or a catered meal before it. For my family, having a connection might not solve all problems, but it helps makes the world, one's station within it—or perceived lack thereof—a bit more bearable.

"All right. Let's go guys."

"Go where, Dad?" JoJo said. "How about Pizza first? I'm starving."

Tony raised an eyebrow. "Pizza? I just told you. We got free food coming our way."

"What kind of food, Dad?" Nino asked.

"Are you kidding?"

Tony looked at me. "These kids, they're frickin burnt, man."

The five of us crammed into Tony's crimson Suzuki Jeep, and off we went. We hit traffic at 11:30, which was teeming with SUVs and station wagons.

Once we got onto the Southern State Parkway, we dodged and weaved in and out of lanes with surprising quickness, to my stomach's dismay. We were about half a mile away from the ballpark when traffic had stopped cold.

"Told you we should've stopped for pizza, Dad," Nino said. "The game's gonna have already started by the time we get there."

"No problem," Tony said. "Watch this, Joey," he said to me. Here's a bold move."

He gripped the wheel and curved the truck out of line and hit the gas, as if he was Michael J. Fox in *Back to the Future*, flooring the DeLorean, so that we would push the flux capacitor to 87 miles per hour. Where we were going, we didn't need roads.

"Hit it, Dad," JoJo yelled.

"Almost there, guys."

Then he turned on the tape deck. The chorus from Boz Scaggs' "What Can I Say" warbled from the speakers.

Beth and I grabbed each other's hand. We sped up to the front of the line, where there was an ever-so-slight opening. Tony merged into it with quick ease, which was received by a cacophony of honking horns and muffled voices of people shouting from rolled down car windows. What can I say, indeed.

"No problem," Tony said. "I know a good place to park."

He found a spot about 50 yards away from the back of the centerfield fence. There were only a few other cars there, to his delight.

"Okay everyone. Let's get to the buffet."

"Don't you think we should get our tickets first, Dad?" Nino asked.

"Whattya think we're doin'? Knitting sweaters?"

Beads of sweat slid down my face. Then Tony smiled a sly little smile. "Don't worry, Joey. Lunch is on the way."

*　*　*

We strode to the "Will Call" booth. "Hi, someone left tickets for me and my family here," Tony said to the teenaged girl behind the booth.

"You're using someone else's tickets?"

"My friend left them for me."

"Under what name?"

"Tony. Look for Tony."

"Let me see what I can find. Oh, here they are. 5 tickets for 'Tony.'"

"That's us," Nino said.

"That's me, buddy," Tony said. "I'm gonna call the fire department, because you're burnt."

What the preserve in the lake was to Casey, the buffet area was to those of us at Citibank Park: we were somewhere that was not intended for us. It was above centerfield and seemed to have the area of four or five tract housing living rooms. Other than two lined trash cans and a "Ducks" rug in the middle of the concrete floor, it was compiled of several card plastic tables, like the kind sold in Staples, Office Depot, or any office supply store, which were just being covered in green, orange, black, and white paper tablecloths, after the Ducks' team colors.

Five gray plastic catering trays flanked the table. They were bookended by two plastic bowls: one with what looked like a standard green salad, the other with Bubblegum-pink watermelon, jaundiced pineapples, and purplish grapes.

We walked slowly into the area, which was clear of people, save us and two people dressed in white shirts, black bowties and dress pants. They were both girls and had big, curly brunette hair. They looked as if they had been sucking lemons.

"Here we go. Let's eat," Tony said.

Beth walked up to the table. "Hi. Excuse me," she said to one of the servers. "Do we just help ourselves?"

"Well, it's a buffet, isn't it?"

I grabbed a Chinet clear plastic plate and scanned the trays. The first one had the saddest looking collection of hot dogs I have ever seen. Their grill marks looked more painted on than cooked, as if made by a food artist for a TV commercial, rather than consumption. What's more, they were slick, as if rubbed in canola oil. My stomach let out a roar that would have made Godzilla proud.

"Good, huh?" The other server asked me.

Beth grimaced. "I'm going to check out the fruit situation," she said.

Nino looked over my shoulder. "Uncle Joey! Something died on your plate."

"Wait until you see the corn on the cobs. They're like punishment on a tray," JoJo said.

I spotted the corn, at the end of the table. They were regular cobs, supposedly from a local farmer. If such was the case, something went terribly awry on their journey to the tray. The cobs were cut in half and were sickly. To say that they were jaundiced would have been an improvement. They tasted like dilapidated firewood logs that were drowned in margarine and water from the East River.

Nino picked one of the cobs up with a plastic fork. "What the hell is this?"

Then his fork snapped. The nub of corn splashed down into the ocean of buttery salt water in the tray.

"How dreadful," I said to Nino.

JoJo was also unimpressed. "Who did they think was coming today? Snow White and the seven dwarfs?"

"I dunno," Nino replied. "Even Dopey wouldn't eat this."

We met Beth by the fruit bowl. "Look," she said to us. She pointed above the bowl.

A halo of flies hovered above the bowl. "I feel like I'm in an Alfred Hitchcock movie," she said.

"Look," Nino said, pointing to another table adjacent to the salad bowl. "Cookies. And soda! Here we go."

Ah, soda. Something that couldn't be messed up. I was excited to see that they had two-liter bottles of RC Cola, which I hadn't had since I was a child. The cookies were as big as our faces, and had chocolate chips and M&Ms peeking out of them like edible, colorful headstones. Nino, JoJo and I took a cookie apiece, and filled our cups with RC.

The three of us met Beth and Tony at a nearby picnic table, where they picked at their meals: Tony at his hot dog buried in sauerkraut and deli mustard and salad, Beth with her tiny bowl of fruit salad.

"Where's your hot dogs, guys?" Tony asked. "No corn? Is that RC Cola? They still make that?"

I took a sip and coughed. My lungs felt like they were on fire.

"Nope. Not for several years," Beth said.

"Cookies? Soda? Nino! Joey! You guys gotta have more than that."

Nino and I bit into our cookies. I felt nauseous instantaneously. I can't speak for Nino's cookie, but mine tasted like burnt sand, with arsenic substituted for sugar. I ran to the trash and nearly had a Technicolor yawn.

Tony took a bite of his hot dog. The color left his face as quickly as he had sped into the front of the line of cars driving into the ballpark parking lot.

"Holy shit! It's like biting into a Firestone tire."

"Firestone?" Nino asked. "Not Dunlop?"

"I mean, I'm gonna write a letter of complaint," Tony said. "This was supposed to be 'world-class' cuisine. I brought my family with me and everything. This is embarrassing."

"Who gave you the tickets, Dad?" JoJo asked.

"Don't worry about it "Let's find our seats."

Our seating situation was far superior to our buffet one. We were about five rows behind the third base line, which gave us a terrific view of the game. Specifically, I marveled the sight of Erick Almonte, a former New York Yankees prospect, whose biggest claim to fame was filling in for Derek Jeter for three weeks during the 2003 season. He was solid at the dish, having hit .260 with a homerun and 11 RBI's in 100 at bats over 31 games played. Unfortunately, Almonte had also made 12 errors in 128 chances, for a .906 fielding percentage, which is substandard for a Major League shortstop. His lackluster defensive game drove some Yankee fans to call him E6, which refers to an error made by a shortstop in baseball scorekeeping parlance. I felt ambivalent about Almonte, but I was curious to see how he would do, given his return to New York as a professional baseball player.

A ball was hit Almonte's way, which promptly went through his legs. I couldn't help but wonder how my father would have reacted. Fortunately for me, others were glad to fill the void.

"Hey Almonte! You're worse than an IRS audit!"

"Hey Almonte! Your ass is bigger than your yard!"

"Hey Almonte! Good news! Target's hiring!"

Fortunately, the Ducks got the next three outs. I don't remember who led off, but the next two Ducks batters reached base, and the following batter struck out on three pitches, leaving Elvis Peña, the Ducks' centerfielder, to come to the dish with runners in scoring position.

Elvis had a cup of coffee with the Colorado Rockies and the Milwaukee Brewers at the end of the 2000 and 2001 seasons, respectively. He was a speedy centerfielder and was batting .285 for the Ducks as of this particular day, at least until this at bat, where hit into an inning ending double play.

"Hey Elvis! Go back to Graceland," JoJo yelled.

"You hit like my grandmother," Beth shouted.

"And she's dead," Nino yelled.

Then we were all silent. The sting of Nonna Ida's absence was made all the more painful by my father's, which reminded me of how incomplete my family had felt to me in the past year. Unlike Nonna Ida, he was still alive, and the reason why we were gathered at the ballpark in the first place.

Looking back, there was more to my reaction to the buffet than a curious lack of flavor. My family and I had the mother of all meals after Nonna Ida's funeral. Nicole had made arrangements for us to eat at a bistro in Queens, which specializes in family-style Orsognese cuisine. We celebrated Nonna Ida's life with an eight-course meal of antipasto, calamari, risotto, roasted pork, eggplant Parmesan, freshly made linguine in Pomodoro, pizza for the children, and endless supplies of fruit, semolina bread, and bottles of wine. This meal was as vibrant as Nonna Ida herself; almost as tasty as her cooking for a standard Sunday Dinner or Christmas Day feast.

While only some branches of the living members of my family tree speak the mother tongue, the chief source of my family's joy and pride in our heritage is in the food we share with one another. When a meal isn't to someone's liking during family gatherings, it almost feels like an affront, whether the get-together in question takes place at someone's residence, a restaurant, or a baseball game.

Then Almonte came to bat. He hit a bloop single over the first baseman, which got the crowd roaring, especially "Quacker Jack," the Ducks mascot, who started doing the chicken dance behind the third base line.

"That's foul, Quacker Jack," a fan behind me yelled. "Foul."

"Imagine if he ate from the buffet," JoJo said.

I yelled, "Let's go Red Wings!"

Nino laughed. "Aren't the Red Wings a hockey team, Uncle Joey?"

In that moment, I wanted to tell Nino how much I missed Nonna Ida, that I wished that my mother, father, brother, Nicole, and Nicky were with us, just so I could have a semblance of so-called normality in my familial life, that I wanted everyone to be together without any acrimony or excuses, if only for the length of the ballgame.

But instead, I went in a different direction, like Almonte and Pena in their respective professional baseball careers.

"The way the Ducks are playing, it might as well be a National Hockey League game," I said. "So let's go Red Wings."

"Let's go Red Wings," Nino yelled.

"Let's go Red Wings," JoJo joined in, as did some other people sitting near us.

Tony smirked and shook his head. "You're burnt, Joe."

I kept cheering until I heard part of the Spinners' song "I'll Be Around" echoing through the ballpark. My thoughts of Nonna Ida and my parents were mustard stains on my Captain America t-shirt.

* * *

Beth and I moved to our current Western New York digs a few years later. The relocation was well received by everyone in our family, with the exception of Casey. He clearly missed the pond, which is to say that he missed chasing after ducks and geese; rolling around in mud and feces; pissing on his favorite pine tree. Fortunately, there were lots of birch and poplar trees in our new neighborhood; lots of new scents for Casey to sniff.

Shortly after we settled into our new digs, he began having fainting spells. He pranced and sniffed as usual, only to fall onto his side, panting moments later.

A veterinarian gave us some bad news. X-rays had shown that Casey had a tumor on his heart. "His days are numbered," was how the veterinarian put it.

He was put on some medication, which stabilized his condition. He only fainted once within three months. We thought that he was getting better.

No such luck. Although Casey still pranced and sniffed, he gradually walked and ran around less, but it didn't stop him from trying to do so. He never failed to scratch our legs when he wanted to sit in our laps or lick sleepers out of the corners of our eyes every morning.

Then he coughed up blood in the middle of a late-March night. We took him to a nearby animal hospital, where he died in his sleep.

Rain is abundant in Western New York. Sometimes I watch it fall on the grass outside my building, and I think of the Ohio yard and pond. The ice is thawed. If I look closely enough, I can see Casey again, standing on the muddy shoreline, his eyes locked on the geese, gliding to and from the reserve.

Extinction Wednesday

What smell is to some people, music is to me. It triggers my memory like nothing else, especially when I listen to it in my car.

Gerry Rafferty's hit song "Baker Street" made me aware of this a few weeks ago, when I was stuck in rush hour traffic. I recalled a Wednesday evening of my childhood. It was April. My family and I were driving on Route 110. Baker Street grooved from the radio of my father's gold-green Pinto station wagon. Raphael Ravenscroft's saxophone's riff glistened in Orion's belt in the otherwise cloudy Long Island sky.

There used to be a drive-in movie theatre that could be seen from Route 110. It was called The Farmingdale Drive-In: it had only one screen, which was always alight with images during the spring and summer months of my childhood.

This night's images were especially thrilling, because I saw two familiar faces dominating the screen: the characters Cornelius and Zira, from the Planet of the Apes: the POTA film franchise. I felt my eyes bulge out of their sockets.

"Mom! Dad! Look! There's Cornelius! And Zira," I shouted. "I really wanna see that movie! Can we go see it? Pleasepleaseplease?"

POTA is an important film in my family's history. My mother claimed that it was the first film she and my father saw as a married couple. My father claimed that my big sister Nicole was made the morning after they saw it. Nicole claimed that our parents didn't know what they were talking about. She still does.

Nicole also introduced me to the original film, having watched it with me on TV a few years earlier. We spent many Saturday afternoons looking and listening to her Talking View Master reels of the 1970's TV show version of POTA, and I actually slept with my action figures of Cornelius and Zira instead of Teddy Bears, which always made my father shake his head and my mother grin.

Nicole and I stared at the drive-in screen, and our parents conferred quickly.

"Ok, sports fans," our father said. "Let's go see what Cornelius and Zira are up to."

My jaw hit the plastic car mat. It was unlike our parents to act with spontaneity with regards to hanging out with me and Nicole. They planned family outings with painstaking attention to detail. We usually went out to dinner and saw a movie together on Saturday night. That we did so on a Wednesday, on a *school night* for Nicole and I, and a work night for my parents, made our impromptu trip to the drive-in all the more curious to me.

Maybe our parents' decision had something to do with the copious amounts of Sangria they consumed during dinner. Or perhaps they didn't want to hear me carrying on about Cornelius and Zira more than they already had. I couldn't be sure of why our parents were amenable to my request, but there our father was, pulling the Pinto into the drive-in entrance.

We got our speaker and found a spot in the theatre lot, where I read the screen: Beneath the Planet of the Apes, which my father referred to as "Beneath."

"Wow," I shouted. "Another Planet of The Apes Movie! Cool!"

"That's right," my father said. "This one picks up where the original left off. Your mother and I saw Beneath years ago, just before you popped out of her uterus. Right, Marie?"

He reached in a bag of Wise potato chips and stuffed a handful of them in his mouth. My mother rolled her eyes.

"Sure Joe," she said. "Take human bites."

My eyes widened as Beneath started. I was intrigued to see that it opened with scenes from POTA, including its famous ending, where the characters Taylor and his companion, the mute Nova discover the

Statue of Liberty, buried in the sand. This makes Taylor realize that he has returned to Earth and that apes have evolved from humans. He then falls to his knees in the sand, shouting "You maniacs! You blew it up! Damn you! God damn you all to hell!" Nova looks at him quizzically, not knowing what she's looking at, or why Taylor is as devastated as Liberty Island.

I, too, was confused. There was a character I had not seen before, an Astronaut named Brent, who was portrayed by James Franciscus. Brent looked like a shorter version of Taylor, and while watching him bury his captain made him come across as a noble person, I was thrilled when Nova showed up on horseback, albeit without Taylor. Brent spotted her and proceeded to interrogate her.

I remember sympathizing with Nova, especially when Brent grabbed Taylor's dog tags, dangling from her neck, as he demanded an answer to his question about where she got them. I cried when I saw the pained expression in her eyes. My mother's face often looked the same way when she was on the phone with my Nonna Ida: her mother.

I stopped crying once Brent stopped talking. Nova's thoughts of Taylor resonated in piano chords as she and Brent strode towards Ape City; the sun a watchful eye as they left a trail of hoofprints in the red, grainy ground.

Noises flew out of my mouth as fast as Brent's spacecraft had traveled through time and space. I oohed and aahed as his and Nova's search for Taylor took them to the remains of a subway station. I pointed at the screen when Brent saw "Queensboro Plaza" tiled into the station wall; when a humming sound led them to St. Patrick's Cathedral, where there was a fountain that filled itself with fresh drinking water; when Brent made a cup with his hands and drank from it. I remember going home and trying it for myself in my family's bathroom sink.

I also got a kick out of General Ursus' hat and his New York accent. Cornelius and Zira were as eloquent and clever as ever. Dr. Zaius did his best to keep the faith. I marveled the mutants, who wore rubber masks and had a religious ceremony, where they sang hymns of thanks and praise of an atomic bomb and the almighty fallout. Sunday mass at my church was never quite like this.

The rest of Beneath held my attention, but the ending floored me. Of all of its twists and turns, the one that kicked me in the shins was when Nova yelled, "Taylor" and was shot and killed by a gorilla soldier. She died just after she discovered her voice.

Nicole held my hand. The shock and sadness I felt from Nova's death was exacerbated by the sight of Taylor's blood-stained hands, which activated both, the atomic bomb and a wellspring of tears that I never knew I had.

Then I was confused by the somber voice over which informed the rest of the audience and me that, "a green and insignificant planet" was "now dead." I wondered who was speaking, given that the world had been destroyed. I wondered if this was supposed to be the voice of God, so I crossed myself.

"I can't believe that Nova, Zira, and Cornelius were killed off," I said to Nicole. "What a lousy ending."

My mother told me that Beneath was "only a movie." My father lit a new smoke. Nicole reminded me that I had my action figures of Cornelius and Zira.

"Don't worry, Jojo," she said. "You can make up your own stories about them. You can use the dolls you have."

"Action figures, Cola," my father said to Nicole. "I'll play with you Joefish. I'll be Captain Kirk. He can lend Zira his phaser. Fuck Klingons."

"God dammit, Joe," my mother said. "Language!"

"I'm sorry. *Forget* Klingons. They're Jerkwaters. Long live William Shatner."

I felt comforted and started considering the creative possibilities I could explore with my dolls/action figures. The thought of Zira teaming up with my Lieutenant Uhura, and Princess Leia action figures in an attempt to save Captain Kirk, Iron Man, Yoda, and Cornelius from the evil clutches of The Joker, Green Goblin, and Boba Fett lifted my spirits. None of them spoke like the human doll Cornelius found in a cave in POTA, but the fate of the world hung in the balance, and I had a say in how the situation might be remedied.

* * *

An office building stands where the drive-in screen used to. Nicole and I drove past it last summer. I thought about the people behind its shiny windows, working to earn their paychecks, heating and eating their lunch in break rooms, or checking their phones; making and confirming plans for the night or weekend. I also wondered if the invisible people were as exhausted as my parents were when they came home from work; how much longer the building would be there.

I drink water with my hands from time to time. When I do so, it conjures images of Brent, which in turn makes me think of Nova, Cornelius, and Zira. I hear Ursus speak. I laugh. I hear Nova speak. I sigh. I see Nicole and our parents, sitting in the Pinto station wagon in all of its green-gold glory, our faces bathed in the gleam of the drive-in screen. I hear Baker Street, crackling on the radio. Gerry Rafferty sings. Raphael Ravenscroft's saxophone's riff crunches in lake effect snow underneath my tires as I take my final turn home.

Notes

The Sylvester Stallone quote comes from the 1979 film *Rocky II*, which was written and directed by Sylvester Stallone.

The Marisa Frasca quote comes from her poetry collection *Wild Fennel*, which was published by Bordighera Press in 2019.

"May Stars" uses dialogue from the 1982 film *E.T.: The Extra Terrestrial*, which was written by Melissa Mathison and directed by Steven Spielberg.

"Orsogna Woman" uses dialogue from the 1978 film *Superman: The Movie*, which was written by Robert Benton, David Newman, Leslie Newman, and Mario Puzo.

"Mikey and His Constipated Five" uses lyrics from the song "Groovin'," which was written by Felix Cavaliere and Eddie Brigati. The song appears on The Rascals' album of the same name, when they were known as the Young Rascals. Atlantic Records released *Groovin'* in 1967.

"Gonna Cry Now" uses dialogue from *Casablanca* (1942), written by Julius J. Epstein, Philp G. Epstein, and Howard Koch and directed by Michael Curtiz. The essay also uses dialogue from *The Godfather Part II* (1974), written by Francis Ford Coppola and Mario Puzo and directed by Francis Ford Coppola; *Dog Day Afternoon* (1975), written by Frank Pierson and directed by Sidney Lumet; and *Rocky* (1976), which was written by Sylvester Stallone and directed by John G. Avildsen.

"Biggs' Deal" uses dialogue from The Art of Star Wars: Episode IV: A New Hope, which was edited by Carol Titleman and includes the complete script of the 1977 film Star Wars, which was written and directed by George Lucas. The Art of Star Wars: Episode IV: A New Hope was published by Del Rey/Ballantine Books in 1997.

"This Means Something" uses dialogue from the 1977 film *Close Encounters of the Third Kind,* which was written and directed by Steven Spielberg.

"Kentucky Fried Idiot" uses dialogue from the 1979 film *Rocky II,* which was written and directed by Sylvester Stallone.

"The Bronze Age" uses dialogue from the 1966 film *Batman: The Movie,* which was written by Lorenzo Semple, Jr., and directed by Leslie H. Martinson. This essay also uses dialogue from the *Batman* TV episode *The Penguin's Nest,* which was written by Lorenzo Semple, Junior, and directed by Murray Golden. This episode originally aired on December 7th, 1966, on the ABC television network.

"Wine and Shine" uses dialogue from the 1980 film adaptation of Stephen King's novel *The Shining,* which was written by Diane Johnson and Stanley Kubrick. The film was directed by Stanley Kubrick.

"Don't Change" takes its title and uses lyrics from the INXS song of the same name, which was written by Andrew Farriss and Michael Hutchence. The song appears on their album *Shabooh Shoobah,* released in 1982 by ATCO Records, which is an imprint of Atlantic Records.

"People of Faith" uses lyrics from the Eurythmics song "Sweet Dreams (Are Made of This)," which was written by Annie Lennox and David A. Stewart. This song appears on the studio album of the same name, which was released by RCA Records in 1982. The essay also uses lyrics from the Michael Jackson song "Beat It," which is on the studio album *Thriller,* released in 1982 by Columbia Records.

"Catch You Later" uses dialogue from the 1983 film *Blue Thunder,* which was written by Dan O'Bannon and Don Jakoby, and directed by John Badham.

All baseball statistics come from www.baseballreference.com.

"Why Not Fred?" uses information from Legends of Hockey: The Official Site of The Hockey Hall of Fame, https://www.hhof.com/HonouredMembers/ MemberDetails.html?type=Player&mem=P200302&list, https:// thehockeywriters.com/docs/butch-goring/, and *The Hockey News* article "Former Islanders Play By Play Broadcaster Took the Art to Its Highest Level," which was written by Stan Fischler and published online in The Hockey News: New York Islanders, on May 29th, 2023.

This essay is also dedicated to the memories of Paul "Motormouth" Blair (1944-2013) and Derrel McKinley "Bud" Harrelson (1944-2024).

Information used in "Assassins Hours" comes from *Greatest Hockey Legends.com: The Hockey History Blog* article "Nick Fotiu," which was written by Joe Pelletier and published on March 1, 2007 at http:// nyrangerslegends.blogspot.com/2007/03/nick-fotiu.html. The essay also uses lyrics from the Tears for Fears song "Head over Heels," which was written by Roland Orzabal and Curt Smith. This song is taken from the studio album *Songs from the Big Chair,* released by Mercury Records in 1985.

"Other Plans" uses lyrics from the Dion and the Belmonts song "I Wonder Why," which was written by Melvin Anderson and Ricardo Weeks. This song was originally released as a .45 RPM by Laurie Records in 1958.

"Going to Fishbein's" uses dialogue from "In Search of the Man-Wolf!" issue 190 of *The Amazing Spider-Man.* Marv Wolfman wrote its script. The artists of this issue were: John Byrne, who created the layouts; Jim Mooney, who did the finishes; Al Milgrom and Keith Pollard, who collaborated on the cover; Jim Novak, who was the issue's letterer; and

Michelle Wolfman, who was the colorist. This comic was published by Marvel Comics on March 10th, 1979.

"Ducks and Geese" uses lyrics from the Boz Scaggs song "What Can I Say," written by Boz Scaggs and David Paich, and appears on the album *Silk Degrees,* released by Columbia Records in 1976.

"Extinction Wednesday" uses dialogue from the 1970 film *Beneath the Planet of the Apes,* which was written by Paul Dehn and directed by Ted Post.

Acknowledgments

Many thanks to the editors of the journals in which the works below previously appeared, sometimes in different versions:

Elm Leaves Journal: Bafangool Day

Long Island Literary Journal: Wine and Shine

Longridge Review: Extinction Wednesday

Ovunque Siamo: Dual Role, May Stars, Orsogna Woman

Wildflower Muse: Other Plans.

I am immensely grateful to Nic Grosso for his generosity and commitment to this book and to everyone else at Bordighera Press for their support of Italian American scholars and writers. Grazie di cuore.

Several rounds of thanks are also due to the fantastic community of writing and friendship that is as essential to me personally as it is to this book's existence: Alegria Garcia, George Guida, Phil LeClare, Baruch November, Samuele Pardini, Lee Romer Kaplan, and Domenica Ruta. I am filled with appreciation and admiration for all of you.

I am also indebted to all of my SUNY Buffalo State colleagues and students. Thank you for collaborating with me and for making our campus such a dynamic, wonderful community to imagine, work, learn, and grow in. Go Bengals, indeed.

The best part of my life is who I am absurdly fortunate to share it with. Endless love, gratitude, and praise to my dearest ones: Roxy, Stella Bella, Max, and Beth. Thank you for being my family. Thank you for loving us as much as I do. My heart is all yours, always.

About the Author

A first-generation Italian American, JOEY NICOLETTI was born in New York City and raised on Long Island. He is the author of ten poetry collections, including *Breakaway* (Broadstone Books, 2023), *Fan Mail* (Broadstone Books, 2021), and *Boombox Serenade* (BlazeVOX

Books, 2019). Joey's poems, essays, reviews, and articles have appeared in numerous journals and anthologies, including *The Rumpus, The Adroit Journal,* and *Drawn to Marvel: Poems from the Comic Books.* He is the Reviews Editor of *VIA: Voices in Italian Americana* and lives with his family in Western New York, where he teaches writing at SUNY Buffalo State. Connect with him on Instagram @joeynicoletti and Twitter @JoeyNicoletti.

VIA FOLIOS

A refereed book series dedicated to the culture of Italians and Italian Americans.

GEORGE GUIDA. *Low Italian*. Vol 41. Poetry.

GARDAPHÈ, GIORDANO, TAMBURRI. *Introducing Italian Americana*. Vol 40. Italian/American Studies.

DANIELA GIOSEFFI. *Blood Autumn/Autunno di sangue*. Vol 39. Poetry.

FRED MISURELLA. *Lies to Live By*. Vol 38. Stories.

STEVEN BELLUSCIO. *Constructing a Bibliography*. Vol 37. Italian Americana.

ANTHONY JULIAN TAMBURRI, Ed. *Italian Cultural Studies 2002*. Vol 36. Essays.

BEA TUSIANI. *con amore*. Vol 35. Memoir.

FLAVIA BRIZIO-SKOV, Ed. *Reconstructing Societies in the Aftermath of War*. Vol 34. History.

TAMBURRI. et al., Eds. *Italian Cultural Studies 2001*. Vol 33. Essays.

ELIZABETH G. MESSINA, Ed. *In Our Own Voices*. Vol 32. Italian/American Studies.

STANISLAO G. PUGLIESE. *Desperate Inscriptions*. Vol 31. History.

HOSTERT & TAMBURRI, Eds. *Screening Ethnicity*. Vol 30. Italian/American Culture.

G. PARATI & B. LAWTON, Eds. *Italian Cultural Studies*. Vol 29. Essays.

HELEN BAROLINI. *More Italian Hours*. Vol 28. Fiction.

FRANCO NASI, Ed. *Intorno alla Via Emilia*. Vol 27. Culture.

ARTHUR L. CLEMENTS. *The Book of Madness & Love*. Vol 26. Poetry.

JOHN CASEY, et al. *Imagining Humanity*. Vol 25. Interdisciplinary Studies.

ROBERT LIMA. *Sardinia/Sardegna*. Vol 24. Poetry.

DANIELA GIOSEFFI. *Going On*. Vol 23. Poetry.

ROSS TALARICO. *The Journey Home*. Vol 22. Poetry.

EMANUEL DI PASQUALE. *The Silver Lake Love Poems*. Vol 21. Poetry.

JOSEPH TUSIANI. *Ethnicity*. Vol 20. Poetry.

JENNIFER LAGIER. *Second Class Citizen*. Vol 19. Poetry.

FELIX STEFANILE. *The Country of Absence*. Vol 18. Poetry.

PHILIP CANNISTRARO. *Blackshirts*. Vol 17. History.

LUIGI RUSTICHELLI, Ed. *Seminario sul racconto*. Vol 16. Narrative.

LEWIS TURCO. *Shaking the Family Tree*. Vol 15. Memoirs.

LUIGI RUSTICHELLI, Ed. *Seminario sulla drammaturgia*. Vol 14. Theater/Essays.

FRED GARDAPHÈ. *Moustache Pete is Dead! Long Live Moustache Pete!*. Vol 13. Oral Literature.

JONE GAILLARD CORSI. *Il libretto d'autore. 1860 - 1930*. Vol 12. Criticism.

HELEN BAROLINI. *Chiaroscuro: Essays of Identity*. Vol 11. Essays.

PICARAZZI & FEINSTEIN, Eds. *An African Harlequin in Milan*. Vol 10. Theater/Essays.

JOSEPH RICAPITO. *Florentine Streets & Other Poems*. Vol 9. Poetry.

FRED MISURELLA. *Short Time*. Vol 8. Novella.

NED CONDINI. *Quartettsatz*. Vol 7. Poetry.

ANTHONY JULIAN TAMBURRI, Ed. *Fuori: Essays by Italian/American Lesbiansand Gays*. Vol 6. Essays.

ANTONIO GRAMSCI. P. Verdicchio. Trans. & Intro. *The Southern Question.*
   Vol 5. Social Criticism.

DANIELA GIOSEFFI. *Word Wounds & Water Flowers.* Vol 4. Poetry. $8

WILEY FEINSTEIN. *Humility's Deceit: Calvino Reading Ariosto Reading Calvino.*
   Vol 3. Criticism.

PAOLO A. GIORDANO, Ed. *Joseph Tusiani: Poet. Translator. Humanist.*
   Vol 2. Criticism.

ROBERT VISCUSI. *Oration Upon the Most Recent Death of Christopher Columbus.*
   Vol 1. Poetry.